Sew Knits
With Confidence

Sew Knits
With Confidence

Nancy Zieman

KRAUSE PUBLICATIONS
Cincinnati, Ohio

Contents

Introduction

It was the late 1960s. The hot topics in the sewing industry were knit fabrics and knit patterns. I was a young girl, just learning to sew. My mom was intrigued with the thought of sewing T-shirts, knit dresses and underwear—yes, tricot undies.

What needle do I use? How do you stitch the seams so they don't pop? Are there pressing pointers? These were the questions asked by sewing enthusiasts. The answers to these questions respectively were: Use a ballpoint needle (a new revelation). Set your machine for a narrow zigzag stitch. And finally, press lightly with a much cooler iron than you're accustomed to using.

Fast-forward almost fifty years. Knit fabrics and knit patterns are enjoying a resurgence in popularity. A greater range of knit fabrics is at our disposal. New sewists are trying knits for the first time and have questions. Others are rediscovering the ease and simplicity of sewing with knit fabrics, but would like a refresher course.

Sew Knits With Confidence is a technique and confidence-building book rolled into one, targeted for any level of knit sewist. Start with the basics and sew a simple knit top. Or, strive to be a designer by adding a flounce to your favorite knit pattern. Sewing confidence is only a page turn away.

Nancy

Chapter 1

Knit Fabrics

Comfy knit clothing is easy to sew and fit, plus knit fabric needs less pressing and care than most other fabric. There is such a variety of knits that basically every hour of a day can be spent in total comfort—pajamas, sportswear, undergarments, workwear and even elegant eveningwear. From lightweight tricot to heavy berber—the gamut is amazing!

Fabric types

Knits are made from natural and/or synthetic fibers. The construction, fabrication and weight determine the type of knit. The blend of fibers, colors and prints is seemingly endless. Knits are comfortable to wear, easy to sew and require very little care. The charisma of specialty knit fabrics is immediate, and the softness unforgettable.

Single knit

Single knits are sometimes referred to as "jersey knits." They are suitable for T-shirts, dresses, pull-on pants and shorts, and sleepwear.

Single knit qualities:

- Lightweight
- 25–50% stretch
- One side of the fabric looks like a knit stitch; the other resembles interlocking loops.
- Single knits have flat vertical ribs on the right side (a lengthwise chain stitch) and horizontal lines (crosswise half-loops) on the wrong side.
- Single knits curl to the right side when pulled on the crosswise grain. This can be an advantage, because it is easy to find the right side when seaming your fabric.
- The surface of single knits is flat and works well for printing.
- Good draping quality is inherent in single knits, and they are somewhat stretchy and resistant to creasing.
- Rayon jersey knits are softer and finer than cotton jersey, but care must be taken when washing because rayon fibers are weak when they are wet.

Stretch types

For all practical purposes, knit fabrications are classified by the amount of stretch that they possess.

Firm stable knits. These knits have very little stretch and may be used much like woven fabrics when choosing a pattern. Some examples are double knit, sweatshirt fleece and raschel knit.

Moderate stretch knits. The typical amount of stretch in a knit considered to have a moderate stretch is about 25%. Some examples of these are single, tricot and interlock knits.

Two-way stretch knits. These knits are quite stretchy and usually include spandex. They stretch in both lengthwise and crosswise directions about 50–75%. Examples include fabrics used for swimwear and bicycle shorts.

Super-stretchy knits. Super-stretchy fabrics may stretch 75–100% in width and 50–100% in length. Examples include slinky knit and knits used for ski wear.

Interlock knit

Interlock knits are a little heavier than single knits and have up to 50% stretch, making them perfect for pants, jackets, tops and sleepwear.

Interlock knit qualities:

- 1×1 knit construction like double knits, but lighter in weight with a soft hand

Note: Because of their construction, interlock knits look the same on both sides—like a very fine rib.

- Usually 100% cotton or a 50/50 cotton-polyester blend
- Stretch on the crosswise grain, but little or no stretch on the lengthwise grain

Note: Pretreat interlock knits before using them, especially those that are 100% cotton, to avoid shrinkage after the clothing is sewn.

Double knit

Double knits are "beefier," or heavier, than single or interlock knits. These knits are great for designs that need more body such as jackets, pants, dresses and skirts.

Double knit qualities:

- Less than 25% stretch
- Firm, medium to heavyweight fabric
- Looks the same on both front and back, like interlock
- Stretch crosswise, but stable lengthwise

Note from Nancy

I make it a rule not to prewash ribbing, even if the fabric has a tendency to shrink. Shrinking in size after making the project will enhance the shaping.

Ribbing

Ribbing has distinguishing vertical ribs on both sides of the fabric and is very stretchy—100% crosswise stretch. Ribbing is typically used to finish necklines, waistlines, armholes, and leg and sleeve hems of mainly knit garments. It is a knit/purl construction.

Ribbing types include:

- **1×1 rib knit**—Knit wales alternate evenly with one on one side and one on the other.
- **2×1 rib knits**—Two wales on one side and one on the other.
- **Baby rib**—Very fine ribbing, usually made with single spun combed cotton fibers. The surface of baby rib is smooth and finer than regular ribbing.

Two-way stretch knit

An elastic synthetic fiber, such as spandex, is generally used in these stretchy knits. Two-way stretch knit is excellent for swimwear, dancewear and other stretchy sportswear.

Two-way stretch knit qualities:

- Spandex is usually blended with polyester, cotton or nylon.
- Stretches in both lengthwise and crosswise directions and has great stretch recovery

Slinky knit

This lightweight stretchy fabric is perfect for travel because it is comfortable to wear, drapes nicely and doesn't wrinkle. This fabric is used mostly in slip-on style dresses, pants, skirts and tops with minimal sewing.

Slinky knit qualities:

- Almost 100% stretch in the width and about 50% stretch in length
- Usually a blend of 90% acetate and 10% spandex

Note: Slinky knit has spandex added to keep clothing from "bagging."

- Has a definite nap—extra fabric is needed to accommodate fabric layout for patterns

Sweatshirt fleece

Sweatshirt fleece generally has one soft, brushed fleece side, and the other side has small, flat vertical ribs. Fleece is very warm and soft next to your skin. Sweatshirts, sweatpants, jackets and other simple sports outfits are often made from sweatshirt fleece.

Sweatshirt fleece qualities:

- Usually 50% polyester and 50% cotton, or 100% cotton
- Lightweight
- Very little stretch in either the length or width

Note: Pretreat sweatshirt fleece before using, especially fleece made of 100% cotton, to avoid shrinkage after the clothing is sewn.

High-loft fleece

Most high-loft fleece is referred to generically as polar fleece, however, the name *Polarfleece* was originally a registered trademark of Malden Mills. This fleece is comfortable, attractive and easy to sew. Use high-loft fleece for sportwear, blankets and craft items.

High-loft fleece qualities:

- Usually 100% polyester or polyester/Lycra blends
- Lightweight
- Similar on each side—almost reversible
- Nonraveling
- Crosswise stretch for wearing comfort

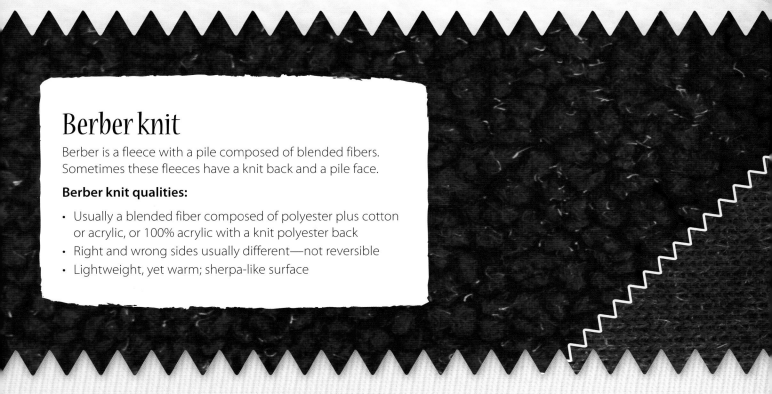

Berber knit

Berber is a fleece with a pile composed of blended fibers. Sometimes these fleeces have a knit back and a pile face.

Berber knit qualities:

- Usually a blended fiber composed of polyester plus cotton or acrylic, or 100% acrylic with a knit polyester back
- Right and wrong sides usually different—not reversible
- Lightweight, yet warm; sherpa-like surface

Tricot knit

Tricot knits are a lingerie mainstay and require minimal sewing.

Tricot knit qualities:

- A warp knit fabric where the yarn zigzags vertically, following a column of the knitting rather than the usual row
- Resistant to runs
- Soft fine knit used for lingerie and sportswear
- Moderate stretch
- Generally 100% nylon

French terry

French terry is lighter than regular terry cloth, making it ideal for children's clothing, robes and beachwear. The textured loop pile is very absorbent, while the smoother side is knit-like and more comfortable against the body. French terry is made with cotton or blends that may contain Lycra for stretchability.

French terry qualities:

- Smooth on one side and uncut loop pile on the other
- A little lighter weight than fleece

Novelty knits

There are many novelty knits, ranging from sheer to heavy. They include French terry, thermal or waffle weave, pointelle, raschel, stretch velour, stretch velvet and more.

Novelty knits may include texture, patterns, spandex and other fabrications to pique interest, or they may have patterns created during the knitting process such as pointelle, waffle/honeycomb and raschel knits.

Thermal or waffle weave

Thermal or waffle knits have a geometric-type texture that looks like a honeycomb pattern and is reversible. Thermal/waffle knits are popular for casual clothing and warm undergarments. This fabric has the look and feel of cotton, but may be 100% spun polyester with the ability to trap heat for warmth.

Thermal or waffle weave qualities:

- Usually made from cotton
- The square textured design traps air to give this fabric its heat-retaining quality.
- Used for outerwear and underwear

Pointelle knit

Pointelle is usually a cotton blend with a tiny openwork pattern. The drop-needle-type stitching gives the fabric its characteristic texture, with the holes forming a design in the knit. Pointelle may be used for children's clothing or feminine adult tops.

Pointelle knit qualities:

- Lightweight openwork knitted design
- Cooler than a solid knit

Raschel knit

Raschel is a warp knit fabric that may have inlaid connecting yarns besides the columns of knit stitches. The fabric looks much like lace, netting or a hand-crocheted fabric. Raschel knits make pretty and feminine tops because of the lacy-type construction features.

Raschel knit qualities:

- Lacelike open construction—resembles hand-crocheted fabrics, lace fabrics and nettings
- A warp knit produced on a multiple-needle knitting machine

Stretch velour

Stretch velour looks and feels like velvet but has the comfort and stretch of a knit when Lycra is added to the fabrication. It's generally made of cotton, but may be made from synthetics, such as polyester. This fabric is most commonly used for dancewear, casual clothing and easy-care upholstery.

Stretch velour qualities:

- Closely cropped pile on the right side of the fabric
- May contain some spandex for extra comfort and fit
- Fuzzy and warm
- Dyes well with fiber-reactive type dyes, which are used mostly for cellulosic fibers (plant based) such as cotton. Colors achieved with fiber-reactive dyes are brilliant and don't fade after repeated washing.

Stretch velvet

Stretch velvet is soft and drapey—it combines the luxury of velvet with the comfort of a knit. This polyester/spandex blend fabric is woven as a double cloth and cut between the layers to form the velvet pile. It is suitable for clothes that drape well and have classic lines, using a minimum of stitching techniques.

Stretch velvet qualities:

- Usually made from rayon or a rayon/silk blend of fiber
- Burnout velvet (shown) is typically created by cutting away the surface pile from velvet in specific areas, leaving a sheer backing to form the design. Or, chemicals may be used to "burn out" the natural fibers and leave behind a polyester sheer knit design.
- Contains spandex for extra comfort and fit
- Dyes beautifully

Weft vs. warp

Knit fabrics fall into two construction categories, weft knits and warp knits. The direction the yarns are looped determines which category a knit is placed in. Most knits are weft knits, combining knit and purl stitches in different ways. The warp knits utilize several yarns that may be looped in addition to the columns of knit stitches. These warp knits may appear lacy or have random loops, depending on the machines they are knit on.

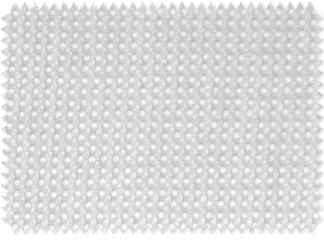

Weft knits

Weft knits use a single yarn looped horizontally to form a row, and each row builds on the previous row. Most knit fabrics fall into this category. Weft knit fabrics may run when cut. There are essentially three groups of weft knits: rib knits (combination of knit and purl stitches), purl knits (purl stitches only), and jersey knits (knit stitches on the front and purl stitches on the back). Some examples of weft knits are single knits, double knits, ribbing and jersey.

Warp knits

Warp knits are made with several yarns that are looped vertically at the same time. Warp knit fabrics produced on multiple-needle knitting machines have a very different structure, and because of the variety of knits that can be produced, may not fall into strict groups as the weft knits do. Tricot and raschel knits are good examples of warp knits.

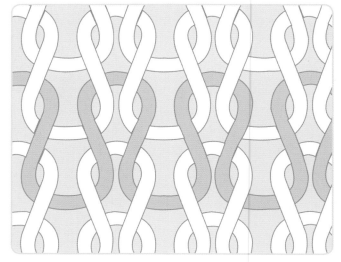

Weft knit

Warp knit

Knit preparation tips

Knits need to be pretreated just as woven fabrics do. Excess finishes need to be removed, and shrinkage needs to be controlled before cutting out the fabric.

Prewash knit fabric using a mild soap or baby shampoo to keep colors bright. It's not necessary to prewash ribbing if the ribbing is the same color as the main fabric.

Prewash ribbing only if the ribbing is a dark color and you are using it on a light colored knit. Prewashing in this situation prevents the color from transferring. Also:

- Cut the ribbing to the correct size before washing.
- Wash with "like" colors. You may also want to use a color-catching laundry sheet to absorb and trap loose dyes in your wash water every time you wash the completed garment.

When pretreating cotton and polyester knits, dry them on a gentle cycle with low heat. Line dry the knit once it is made into clothing. The dryer tends to wear out clothing faster than normal wear and tear.

To remove wrinkles from your knits, fluff them in the dryer for a short time after washing—not drying them completely. Then hang the garments until they are completely dry.

Rayon is weak when wet. Prewash rayon knits using the following guidelines:

- Wash rayons by machine on a gentle cycle with a mild soap. It is best to wash rayons alone and in a mesh bag.
- Line-dry rayons to avoid excessive shrinkage.

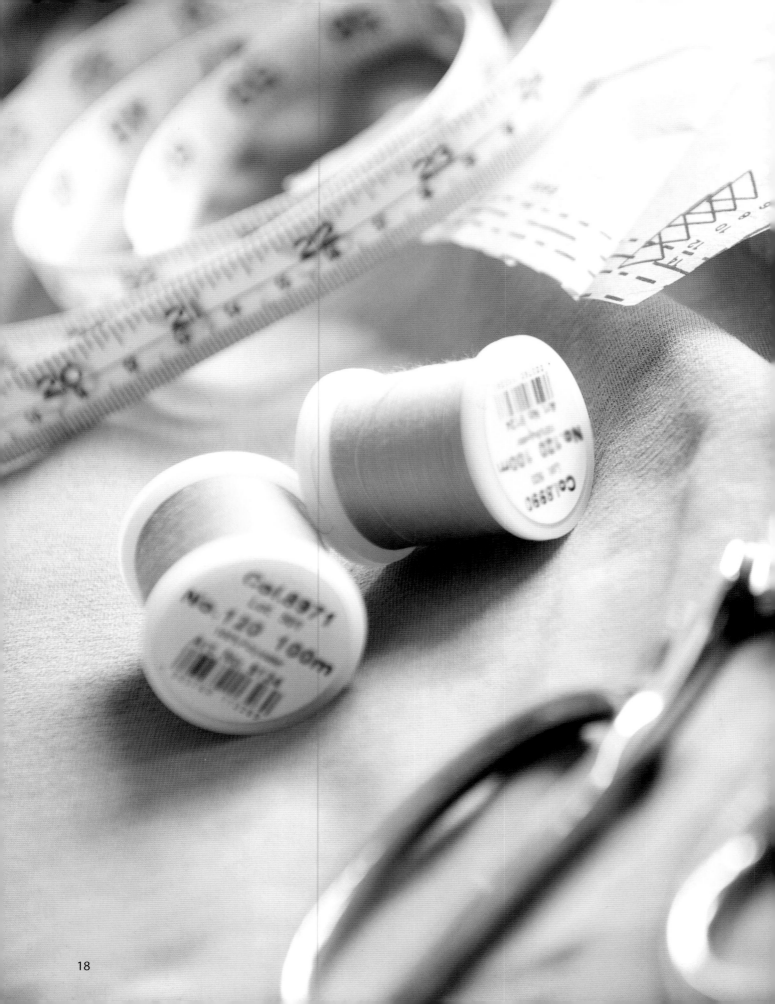

Chapter 2

Patterns and Notions for Knits

Knit patterns generally include simple lines and easy construction techniques. Peruse knit pattern choices and decide on styles that work well for you and the knit fabric you've chosen.

Once you decide on a pattern and fabric, a few simple notions will jump-start the sewing process—stretch needles, good-quality polyester thread, long ballpoint pins and a great pair of shears. However, as the variety of knit fabrics increases, so do the number and kind of notions that make your job easier.

Pattern styles for knits

Use patterns with simple lines, gathers and drapeable fullness, a minimum of buttonholes and other closures, easy hems and necklines, ties, elastic, easy embellishments, and other features complementary to knit fabric with a soft image.

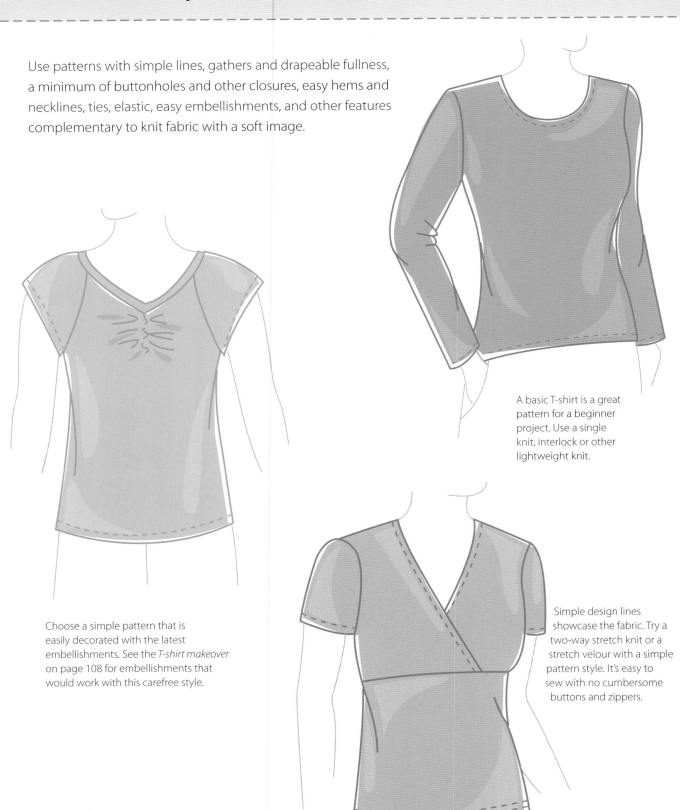

A basic T-shirt is a great pattern for a beginner project. Use a single knit, interlock or other lightweight knit.

Choose a simple pattern that is easily decorated with the latest embellishments. See the *T-shirt makeover* on page 108 for embellishments that would work with this carefree style.

Simple design lines showcase the fabric. Try a two-way stretch knit or a stretch velour with a simple pattern style. It's easy to sew with no cumbersome buttons and zippers.

Hem interlock knits with ease using a double (twin) needle, or use a cover stitch on your serger (see page 69).

Use the elastic casing technique on page 50 when sewing knit pants and straight skirts. Double knits are a great choice—they're a sturdy knit and easy to sew.

Interlock knits and flowing skirt patterns are ideal combinations.

Fleece fabrics are very forgiving to sew. Stitches hide in the nap of the fabric, so if they're a little crooked, no one will notice. Experiment with sweatshirt or polar-type fleeces.

Tricot is fun to sew. You can trim it with peek-a-boo lace, covered elastic, corded piping and picot stitches, for feminine flair.

Knit jackets showcase the fabric. Look for a jacket with simple lines and easy closures.

Attention serger owners! Two-way stretch fabric and the durable overlock stitch are the perfect duo for activewear.

Serge or sew gymnastics or dance outfits for your kids or grandkids. The savings are phenomenal! Polyester/Lycra blends are perfect for activewear, as they take color well and stretch for comfortable movement.

Note from Nancy

Use a serger to stitch seams, trim excess fabric and overlock the edges—all at the same time! A serged seam is stretchy—perfect for swimwear and other two-way stretch knits.

Pairing knit patterns and fabric

Many patterns are designed specifically for knits. They generally allow less wearing ease than those intended for woven fabrics. Selecting an appropriate knit fabric for the pattern you're using is essential.

Different types of knits have different amounts of stretch. Check the pattern. If it lists knits as a suitable fabric choice, it generally includes a printed guide on the back of the pattern envelope indicating how much stretch the fabric must have to be suited for the pattern.

Select an appropriate knit for a pattern by testing the crosswise grain of the fabric (the grain that runs from selvage to selvage).

1. Position a section of the fabric (about 5" [13cm] in from the edge) over the knit guide on the pattern envelope. Securely hold the knit at the left edge of the guide.

2. With your right hand, grasp the fabric at the distance indicated on the fabric (generally 4" [10cm]).

3. Stretch the knit. It must stretch to the second position on the guide to be suitable to use for that particular pattern.

Check the stretch recovery of the knit selected for your pattern by stretching the knit and observing how well it springs back to its original shape.

Trace multi-sized patterns.

1. Select the size you would like to make on the multi-sized pattern.

2. Trace the desired size onto pattern paper.

3. Transfer all markings such as notches, grainline, hem allowance, center front, button placement and any other critical construction details.

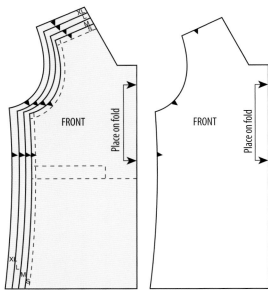

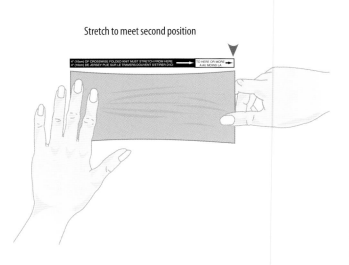

Stretch to meet second position

4" (10cm) OF CROSSWISE FOLDED KNIT MUST STRETCH FROM HERE
4" (10cm) DE JERSEY PLIE SUR LE TRAVERS DOIVENT S'ETIRER D'ICI
TO HERE OR MORE
A AU MOINS LA

Note from Nancy

Be aware of the new wave of fabrics on the market that are stretchy like knits, but aren't really knits at all, such as stretch denim. Stretch denim is a woven fabric with the addition of spandex yarns. You'll need to check these "imposter" knits with the knit guide as well to see if they may be suitable for your pattern.

Note from Nancy

Here's a great tip for using multi-sized patterns. It makes it possible for you to use any of the smaller sizes on the pattern without cutting away the larger sizes. Also, there's no tracing!

4. Cut out the pattern along the marking for the largest size.

To use a smaller size:

- On straight edges, press under the pattern along the marked cutting line using a dry iron.
- On curved edges such as necklines and armholes, clip the pattern edges to the cutting line, allowing you to press under the pattern to the desired cutting line.

To reuse a larger size, simply re-press the pattern.

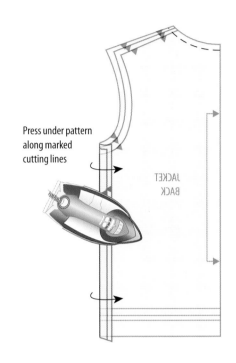

Press under pattern along marked cutting lines

JACKET BACK

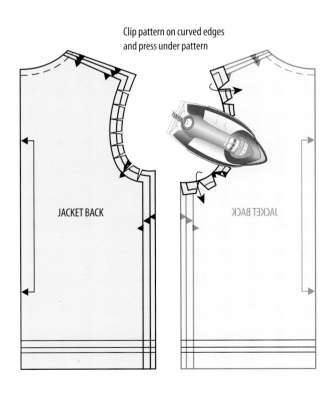

Clip pattern on curved edges and press under pattern

JACKET BACK

JACKET BACK

Notions for knits

A stretch needle and polyester thread are must-have notions for knits, but as you will see, there are many other tools and supplies that not only make sewing knits more enjoyable, but also help you save time and enjoy a professionally finished garment. Sewing knits is simple and fun when you use suitable notions.

Note from Nancy

You might think that all-purpose sewing machine thread and serger thread could be interchanged. Not so! Sewing machine thread has 3 plys (strands) and serger thread has 2 plys. Since three or more cones of thread are used at the same time on your serger, all-purpose sewing machine thread would cause a thick seam. If you were to use one cone of serger thread on your sewing machine, the seam would be weaker.

Thread

All-purpose thread made of 100% polyester or a poly/cotton blend is the best thread to use on your sewing machine when sewing knits. Use a 50 weight/2-ply or 100 weight/3-ply.

All-purpose serger thread made of 100% polyester works well on your serger for serging knits. Use a 40 weight/2-ply cone thread.

Texturized woolly-like serger thread is used in the loopers of your serger. This 100% spun polyester works well for serging soft baby clothing, and it also fills in well when used for rolled edges.

Pins

Ballpoint pins have a rounded tip that won't pierce knit fibers and cause holes. Colored plastic heads make them easy to see and easy to grasp. If you prefer pins to hold your patterns in position and your pattern pieces together, these are the best for knits.

Needles

Stretch needles and ballpoint needles are designed with a medium ballpoint tip that prevents snags on knit fabrics. The ballpoint needle works well on sweater-type knits. The eye and scarf of the stretch needle are specially designed to prevent skipped stitches on highly elastic knitwear such as spandex.

- **For lightweight knit fabric:** Use ballpoint size 70/10 or stretch size 75/11.
- **Medium-weight knit fabric:** Use ballpoint or stretch size 80/12.
- **Heavyweight knit fabric:** Use ballpoint or stretch size 80/12 or 90/14.

Stretch twin needles are designed with the same ballpoint tips as the single-stretch needles to prevent snags. Twin needles share one shank that inserts into your sewing machine. Most zigzag sewing machines can utilize a twin needle. The opening in the throat plate needs to be large enough to accommodate two needles, and your machine must thread from the front to the back.

A twin needle is great for topstitching hems as it stitches two rows of straight stitches on the top of the hem, and the bobbin thread forms a zigzag stitch on the reverse side to build stretch into the hem—this helps keep stitches from popping when the fabric is stretched. The eye and scarf of each of the needles are designed to prevent skipped stitches.

Sizes 3.0, 4.0 and 6.0 are the sizes of twin needles recommended for knits.

Shears and scissors

Micro-serrated shears have tiny teethlike grippers on the lower blade that hold slippery knits as you cut. The slightly blunted points prevent snagging the fabric.

Small scissors or clippers are a good investment no matter what type of fabric you sew. They are handy to clip threads, rip out seams and trim as you sew.

Soft stretch elastic

Buttonhole elastic

Clear elastic

Drawcord elastic

Elastic thread

Fold-over elastic plush

Fantastic Elastic (cut)

Fantastic Elastic (uncut)

Knitted elastic

Lingerie elastic

Elastic for knits

Soft stretch baby elastic, ⅛" (3mm)
- 55% polyester/45% rubber
- Use for necklines and sleeves.
- Insert into casings or stitch directly to wrong side of fabric.

Buttonhole elastic
- 70% polyester/20% nylon/10% spandex
- Use for maternity clothes, children's wear and other adjustable waistbands.

Clear elastic
- 100% polyurethane
- Stretches up to four times its length and returns to its original state
- Use in swimwear, exercise wear and to stabilize seams in knits.

Drawcord elastic
- 66% polyester/34% rubber; 100% polyester drawcord
- Comfortable and adjustable
- Use for shorts, pants and other sportswear.

Elastic thread
- 28% polyester/72% rubber
- Very thin poly-wrapped rubber
- Use to create gathering, shirring or smocking.

Fold-over elastic plush
- 62% nylon/28% polyester/10% spandex
- White, but may be dyed
- Use in place of bias tape or ribbing to finish a neckline on knits, sleeve edges on baby clothes or raw edges on fleece.

Fantastic Elastic
- 1½" (38mm) wide, and can be cut down to ¼" (6mm) width
- No raveling, and stretch isn't compromised when cut

Knitted elastic
- 67% polyester/33% rubber
- Comfortable elastic for sleeves, swimwear, necklines, waistbands and leg bands

Lingerie/picot edge elastic
- 70% polyester/30% rubber
- Stitch directly to wrong side of fabric, allowing decorative edge to show on lingerie and bodysuits.

Rulers and guides

Binding ruler

- Use the 45° angled bottom edge of a binding ruler to cut bias strips (use the straight bottom edge of a quilting ruler to cut crossgrain strips).
- Binding rulers are available in two sizes: 2¼" × 30" (57mm × 76cm) and 2½" × 30" (64mm × 76cm).
- Cut binding strips the perfect width every time without tedious measuring using a binding ruler.

Shape Cut Plus ruler

- Cut strips quickly and accurately using this ruler along with a rotary cutter and cutting mat.
- Cut multiple strips in ¼" or ½" (6mm or 13mm) increments.
- Use the Shape Cut Plus ruler for fringing fabric with ease.
- Cut bias strips for knit trim using the 45° markings to position the fabric.

Pattern weights

Use pattern weights in combination with a cutting mat and rotary cutter to cut out your favorite patterns. Shaped weights and canvas weights are definitely handy helpers designed for the job, but small unopened cans of tuna or veggies make an economical substitute.

Shaped weights conform to the shape of the various pattern curves, corners and straight areas. Shaped weights are smooth, user-friendly and often the perfect weight for holding a pattern in position.

Canvas weights are soft, nonsnagging and colorful. They are fun to use and a good alternative to shaped weights.

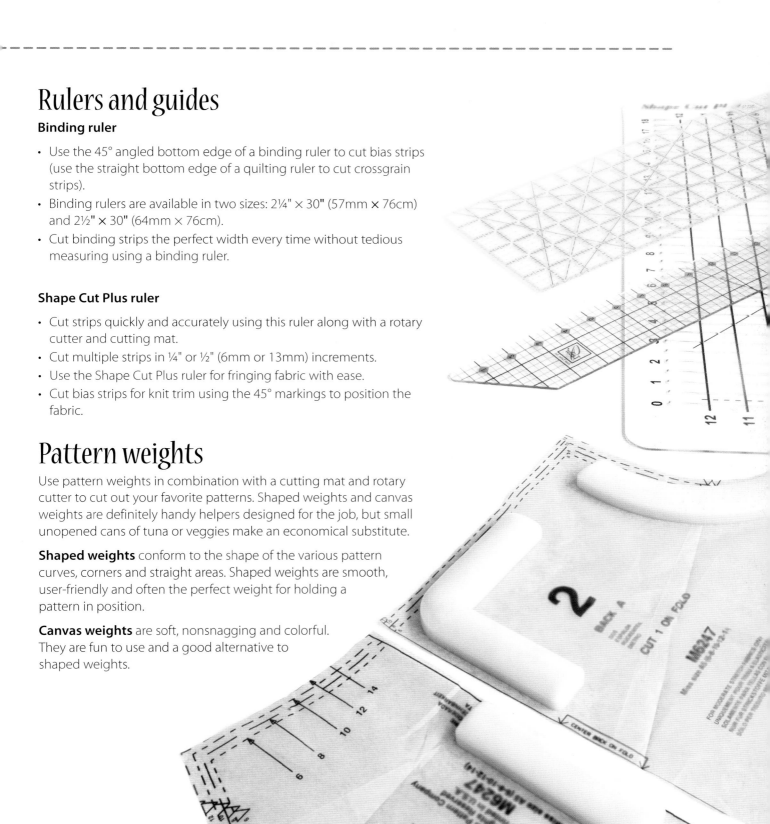

Pattern notcher

The pattern notcher does one thing—cuts slits for notches, but it does it very well and in one step. It is definitely a timesaver, and notches are uniform in size. Plus, you don't need to worry about clipping too far into the seam. It cuts a ¼" × ¹⁄₁₆" (6mm × 2mm) slit in your pattern where your triangular notches are located.

Specialty feet

Overcast guide foot. This foot is designed to help finish or overcast fabric edges without tunneling or stretching. Combine the overcast guide foot with a stretch stitch that overcasts the edges on knits, and you'll have success in seaming knits.

Blind hem foot. Hem your knit fabrics with a blind hem stitch that is almost invisible. This foot helps position and hold fabric straight for a blind hem stitch. A blind hem foot is usually machine specific and may be included in your machine accessories.

Interfacing

Interfacing is typically used to shape collars, cuffs and plackets; to reinforce buttonholes; and to stabilize seams. Knit interfacing is also used to underlie light to medium-weight fabrics. Choose knit interfacing that is:

• 100% polyester knit (comes in white, black or cream)

• 20" or 60" (51cm or 152cm) wide

• Fusible on one side

EASE

6 8 10 12

Fuse 'n Gather tape

Fuse 'n Gather tape (not pictured) is ⅝" (16mm) wide and comes in a 6 or 15 yard (5m or 14m) package. Use it to easily create gathers on dresses, pillows, quilts and crafts. Just press, pull and stitch to gather.

1. Press Fuse 'n Gather tape on the wrong side of the fabric, with the blue threads on the top.

2. Tie the threads at one end.

3. Pull the blue threads at the opposite end of the tape to gather.

Rotary cutters

I prefer to use ergonomic rotary cutters (45mm and 60mm are available) when cutting fabric as there is less stress on your hands, and the ergonomic cutter is comfortable to hold during long cutting sessions.

- Use a **28mm rotary cutter** for cutting out the curved and inner areas of your pattern.
- Use a **45mm rotary cutter** for general straight cutting.
- Use a **60mm rotary cutter** for cutting high-loft fleece, berber and other pile knits.

Cutting mat

A rotary cutting mat is a necessity when using a rotary cutter; it protects the surface you are cutting on from blade marks. Use a mat 24" × 36" (61cm × 91cm) or larger for cutting out large clothing patterns.

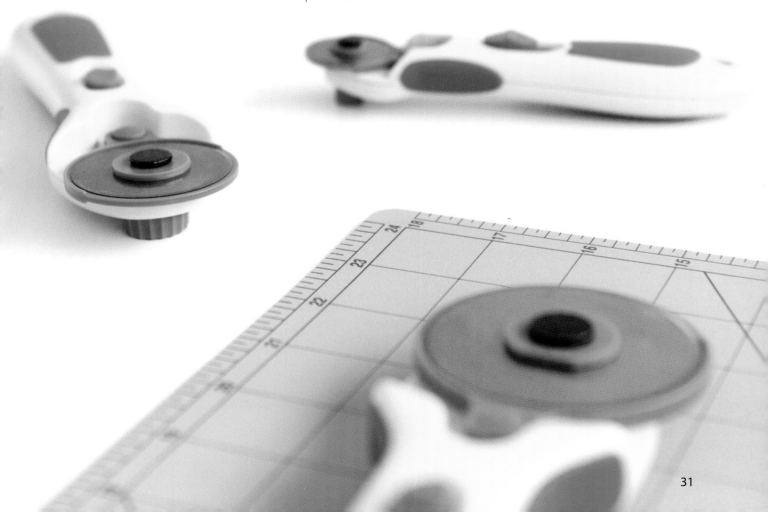

Chapter 3

Basic Knit Techniques

Most of the knit techniques featured in this chapter are tried and true—time-honored traditional knit sewing methods used in the past, but updated for the new knits in the marketplace as well. Both the novice and the accomplished sewist will discover a wealth of speedy sewing and finishing techniques. You'll learn the basics of sewing on knits from start to finish.

Pattern layout for knits

Take care to follow the guidelines below for laying out and cutting your knit pattern pieces. You need to consider the type of knit, pattern guides, positioning pattern pieces, cutting equipment and marking. Jump-start your sewing with a few tips, and you'll sail through your project with finesse.

Lay out the pattern

Be sure to work on a flat surface. To prevent knit fabric from stretching as you cut, make sure to support the full weight of the fabric on the table or cutting board rather than letting any yardage drape over the edge.

1. Place right sides of fabric together before laying out your pattern pieces if the knit fabric has a pile, such as stretch velour. It will be much easier to cut.

2. Use a one-way or nap layout, placing the tops of all pattern pieces so they face in the same direction. You'll see subtle color variations when the nap runs in different directions.

3. Position larger pattern pieces first, starting with those that are placed on the fold. Pin patterns to the fabric fold.

4. Position the remaining pattern pieces on the straight of grain using the pattern grainline arrows. Make sure that the wales of the knit are straight lengthwise.

- Anchor one end of a grainline arrow with a pin; measure from the arrow to the fold, using a 24" (61cm) quilting ruler for ease and speed.

- Adjust the other end of the arrow up or down until the measurement is the same. Pin grainline in place.

- Use pattern weights such as shaped weights or soft canvas weights, page 29, to secure remaining pattern edges. Weights save time, since after cutting one section, you can merely reposition the weights, rather than having to remove and reinsert pins.

Note from Nancy

I like to extend the grainline so it goes the entire length of the pattern. To easily extend the grainline, fold the tissue pattern along the grainline, then press the fold using a dry iron.

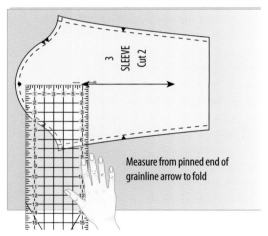

Measure from pinned end of grainline arrow to fold

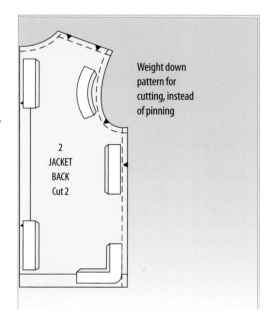

Weight down pattern for cutting, instead of pinning

Cut out the pattern

Shears with a serrated edge are a priority for knit fabrics because they don't slip as you are cutting, even on lightweight fabric such as tricot. End hand fatigue from trying to cut slippery knits with regular shears.

1. Use a dressmaker's shears with a micro-serrated blade. The serrations on these shears grasp the fabric. The slightly blunted points also prevent snagging.

2. Place your left hand (if right handed) on the pattern piece as you cut to keep the fabric in place and prevent shifting.

3. Use long strides as you cut.

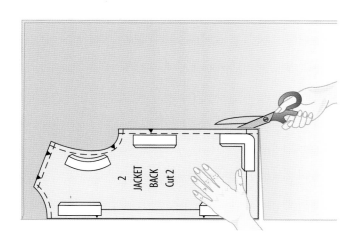

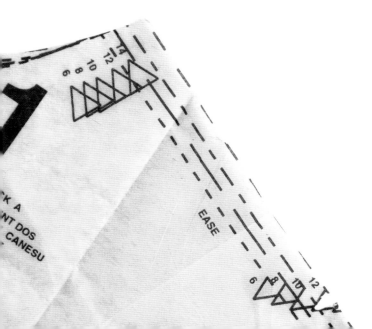

Transfer pattern markings

Water-erasable pens, chalk markers and the pattern notcher are a few of my favorite notions for marking knits. It is critical to mark notches, dots and other parts of the pattern that are used for matching.

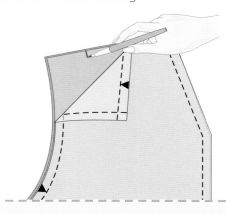

If the pattern includes ¼" (6mm) seam allowances, use a fabric marking pen or chalk to transfer the markings to avoid nipping past the seamline.

If the pattern includes ⅝" (16mm) seam allowances, mark notches with "nips"—short ¼" (6mm) clips into the seam allowance. The pattern notcher also works well for cutting short ¼" (6mm) nips in the fabric (see page 30).

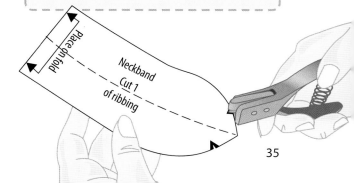

Seams

The beauty of sewing knit seams is that there are very few rules to follow. The sewing is simple whether you are using a sewing machine or a serger—it's a cinch!

Using a sewing machine

Seam with a sewing machine using a ballpoint or a stretch needle, threading the top and bobbin of the machine with an all-purpose polyester or a cotton/polyester thread.

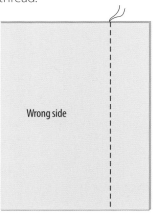

Wrong side

For stable knits, straight stitch the seam with a 3mm–3.5mm stitch length.

For stretchy knits, use two rows of stitching: a straight stitch (3mm–3.5mm), followed by a zigzag. If the pattern includes a ⅝" (16mm) seam allowance, trim the seam allowance to ¼" (6mm).

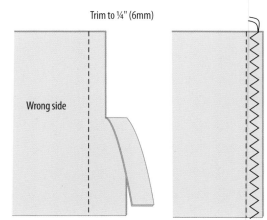

Trim to ¼" (6mm)

Wrong side

Slightly stretch fabric in front and in back of the presser foot as you sew to avoid popped stitches when the fabric is stretched. Stitch another row close to the raw edge to keep seam allowances together.

For knits with greater stretch (50% stretch or more), use a "wobble stitch." This stitch is really important when stitching slinky knits with a conventional sewing machine, but it can also be used on other knits with moderate stretch.

1. Adjust the machine for a zigzag with stitch width set at 0.5mm and stitch length at 1.6mm.

2. Stitch the seam.

Wrong side

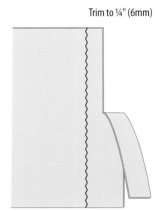

Trim to ¼" (6mm)

Wrong side

3. Optional: Zigzag edges together with a wider zigzag.

Using a serger

Seam with a serger using a 4-thread overlock.

1. Position pins parallel to the seam allowance to avoid hitting the blade mechanism.

2. With ⅝" (16mm) seam allowances, measure ⅝" (16mm) from the needle or refer to your owner's manual. **With ¼" (6mm) seam allowances,** align the edge of the fabric with the blade.

3. Serge, trimming away any seam allowance in excess of ¼" (6mm).

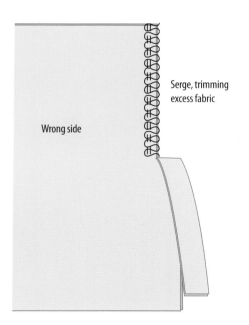

Serge, trimming excess fabric

Wrong side

4. Press knit underarm seams toward the back of the garment, and sleeve seams toward the sleeve.

Stabilizing shoulder seams

Stabilize shoulder seams to prevent them from stretching out of shape. The completed seam can stretch, yet it remains stable with good retention.

1. Cut a piece of clear elastic the length of the seam.

2. Stitch using a wobble stitch (page 36), or serge the seam, including the elastic in the seam.

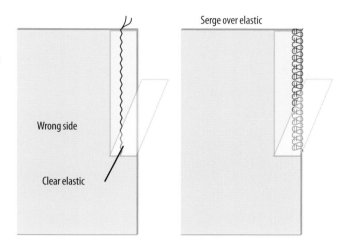

Serge over elastic

Wrong side

Clear elastic

Note from Nancy

For stretchy knits with a two-way stretch, such as swim and dancewear, choose a 3-thread overlock serger stitch with a texturized woolly nylon thread in the loopers.

Interfacings

Interfacing is used to shape collars, cuffs and plackets; to reinforce buttonholes; and to stabilize seams. For knit fabrics, it is important to have a knit interfacing that has some "give" so that the fabric doesn't become too stiff. Shapely and soft is the look to achieve.

Add interfacing

Add interfacing as needed, or as directed on the pattern guide sheet.

1. Choose a fusible knit interfacing such as fusible tricot.

> Don't prewash fusible tricot interfacing in your washing machine, as some of the fusible may wash off. If you preshrink your fashion fabric, preshrink the fusible tricot by dipping it in warm water and letting it air dry.

2. Cut the interfacing the same size as the pattern piece.

3. Fuse the interfacing to the wrong side of the fabric following manufacturer's instructions.

4. Optional: Serge or zigzag the outer edge of the facing to provide a clean finish.

Fabric wrong side

Note from Nancy

I like to use a knit interfacing to keep the knee area from bagging on knit pants, such as interlock, that don't contain spandex for stretch recovery. Here's how:

1. Mark a knee line midway between the crotch line and the hemline.

2. Cut two pieces of interfacing, each 8" (20cm) long and the width of your pant leg at the knee area.

3. Before stitching the leg seams, center interfacing over the front knee area on the wrong side of each of the pant legs, fusible side down.

4. Press into position; stitch leg seams.

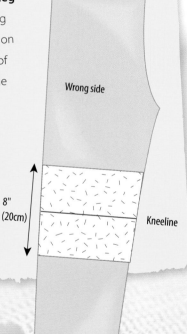

Wrong side

8" (20cm)

Kneeline

Elastics

When you think of your most comfortable skirts, pants and shorts, you are probably already picturing an elastic waistline. Elastic is a mainstay in much of the activewear, sportswear and loungewear on the market because it stretches as your body moves, and it feels loose and casual.

Basic elastic casings

This classic method of applying elastic is fast and easy. Here are some timesaving hints to make the process even easier.

1. Select an elastic. Choose any of the basic types of elastics (see page 28).

2. Cut the elastic about 2"–3" (5cm to 8cm) shorter than the waistline measurement.

3. Form a casing.

- Zigzag or serge the waistline edge.

- Casing widths vary, but a common width is about 1¼" (31mm). Turn under and prepress the casing using a sewing and hem gauge, guiding the iron along the top edge to get an even width. You can prepress this casing either before or after stitching the seam.

- Stitch side, center front and center back seams. On the center back seam, stop and lock stitching at the casing foldline where the casing is turned to the wrong side of the garment. Keeping this area unstitched makes it easier to insert the elastic after the casing is pressed to the wrong side. Press seams open.

- Trim away half the width of the seam within the casing area to minimize bulk.

- Baste the center back seam allowances to the garment for approximately double the width of the casing. This prevents the bodkin or safety pin from getting caught underneath the seam as the elastic is inserted.

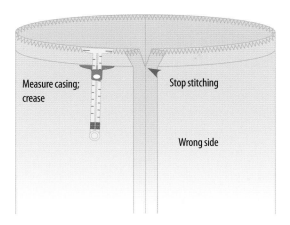

Measure casing; crease

Stop stitching

Wrong side

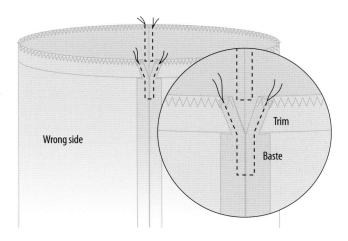

Wrong side

Trim

Baste

- Fold the casing to the wrong side along the prepressed casing line. Pin.

- Stitch around the lower edge of the casing.

- Optional: Also stitch along the top fold to keep the elastic snug. The distance between the two lines of stitching must be slightly greater than the width of the elastic.

4. Insert the elastic into the casing.

- Cut a 2" (5cm) square of firmly woven fabric. Position one cut edge of the elastic over the fabric and securely zigzag the end of the elastic to the fabric. The fabric square helps prevent the free end of the elastic from being drawn into the seam opening. Attach an elastic guide, bodkin or safety pin to the unstitched end of the elastic.

Stitch casing edges

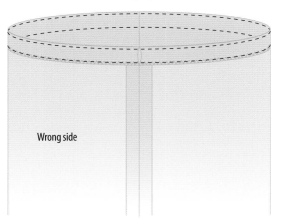

Wrong side

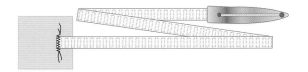

Note from Nancy

Another option is to fuse the seam allowance to the garment with narrow strips of paper-backed fusible web. Fuse the web to the fabric; remove the paper backing; then press the seam allowance to the garment.

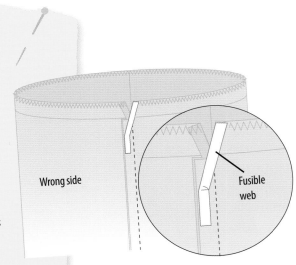

Wrong side

Fusible web

- Thread the elastic through the opening in the seam. Because the seam allowances are secured, the bodkin passes right over them.

- "Kiss" the other end of the elastic against the first end. Unclip the bodkin and zigzag through both the elastic and fabric several times.

- Trim away excess fabric and slide the end of the elastic into the casing.

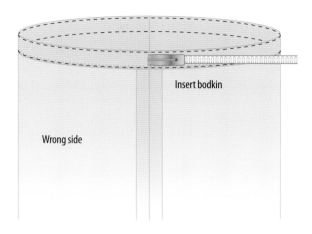

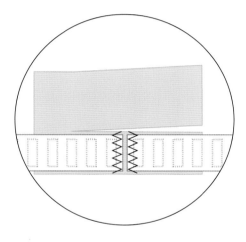

5. If seam allowances were basted in place, remove the basting stitches. Distribute the fullness evenly around the waistline.

Note from Nancy

If desired, you can stitch in the ditch at seams—stitching in the well created where seams meet—to distribute the gathers and prevent the elastic from curling and tunneling in the casing.

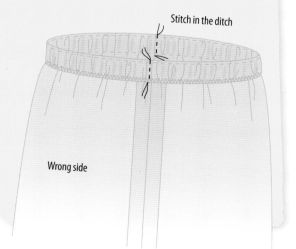

Buttonhole elastic

This ingenious knitted elastic has buttonholes spaced ½"–1" (13mm to 25mm) apart. You'll love this elastic for growing kids' clothes, maternity wear, or whenever you need a little waistline adjustment. We can all use a little waistline adjustment at one time or another! Applying this elastic uses many of the same techniques detailed for a traditional casing. After completing the application, simply rebutton the elastic in a different hole for a more comfy fit whenever you have a slight waistline change.

1. Cut elastic longer than needed for the waistline. The added length is essential to provide room for waistline adjustments. Use a longer length, then cut the elastic to the finished size after threading it through the casing.

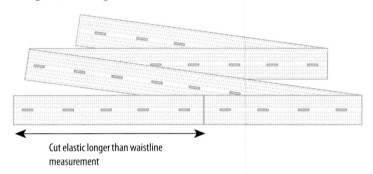

Cut elastic longer than waistline measurement

Note from Nancy

I often don't even cut the elastic until after inserting it into the casing. Then I can be sure I've allowed an appropriate length to accommodate later adjustments.

2. Form a casing.

- Zigzag or serge the waistline edge.

- Turn under and prepress the casing using a hem gauge.

- Stitch the side/center seams, leaving one of the seams unstitched from the foldline to the cut edge.

- Trim away half the width of the seam within the casing area.

- Machine baste each seam allowance to the garment for about 3" (8cm) from the upper edge to prevent the elastic from getting caught under the seam when the elastic is inserted. Or, fuse the seam allowances to the garment using narrow strips of paper-backed fusible web.

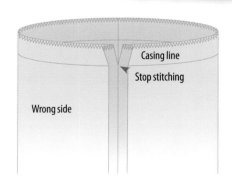

Casing line
Stop stitching
Wrong side

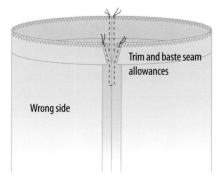

Trim and baste seam allowances
Wrong side

3. Attach a button next to the casing opening.

- Select a button that fits through the elastic's buttonhole openings.

- Unfold the casing. Position the button on the right side of the opened casing, next to the side seam opening.

- Position one end of the elastic on the underside of the casing, under the button. Stitch the button to the casing, sewing through the elastic. The stitching should go through only the casing area.

4. Refold the casing into position. Stitch the casing, sewing completely around its lower edge.

5. Attach a bodkin to the free end of the elastic and insert the elastic through the casing.

6. Pull up the elastic to desired size. Secure the free edge of the elastic to the garment by buttoning it over the button.

7. If desired, conceal the remaining elastic end by tucking it into the unstitched opening.

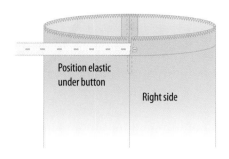

Position elastic under button

Right side

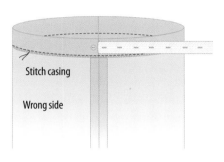

Stitch casing

Wrong side

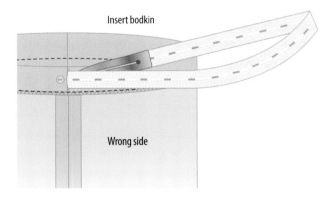

Insert bodkin

Wrong side

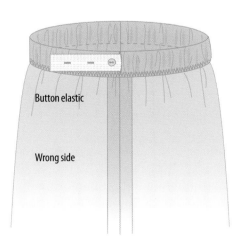

Button elastic

Wrong side

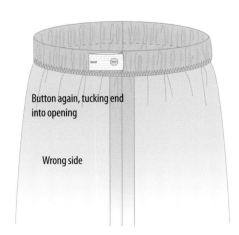

Button again, tucking end into opening

Wrong side

Clear elastic

Clear elastic is ideal for sewing on knits. It's especially good to use on swimwear and children's garments. This ¼" (6mm) or ⅜" (10mm) wide 100% polyurethane elastic stretches up to three times its original length, and easily retracts to its original size.

Use clear elastic to stabilize seams in knit garments. The elastic stretches as you put on or take off a garment, then returns to its original size to hug your body and keep garment shaping intact.

1. Stabilize shoulder seams using one of the following options.

Option 1: Serge the elastic to the garment.

- Cut clear elastic the length of the finished shoulder seam.

- Adjust the serger for a 4-thread overlock. Keep the blade engaged.

- Meet and pin shoulder edges, right sides together. Stitch several stitches.

- Raise the presser foot and place the elastic under the foot, along the seamline. If the pattern allows ⅝" (16mm) seam allowances, be sure to position the elastic over the ⅝" (16mm) seamline.

- Hold the elastic at a slight tension. Do not pull it, but keep it slightly taut. Serge the elastic to the shoulder seam.

Option 2: Stitch to attach the elastic.

- Cut clear elastic the length of the finished shoulder seam.

- Adjust the sewing machine for a wobble stitch (page 36), using a stitch length of 1mm and a stitch width of 1.5mm.

- Position and stitch the elastic to the seam as for the serged application.

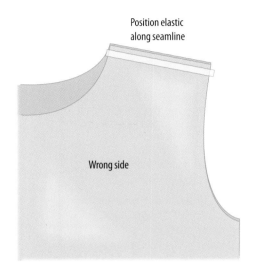

Position elastic along seamline

Wrong side

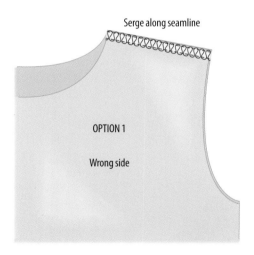

Serge along seamline

OPTION 1

Wrong side

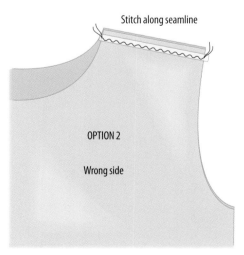

Stitch along seamline

OPTION 2

Wrong side

2. Stabilize neckline seams.

- If the pattern allows a standard ⅝" (16mm) seam, trim the seam allowance to ⅜" (10mm).

- Cut clear elastic the length of the neckline. Position the elastic on the wrong side of the neckline.

- Serge or zigzag the elastic to the neckline. (Disengage the blade if using a serger.) Hold the elastic at a slight tension; you don't want to gather the edge.

- Fold under the elastic. It's not necessary to pin, as the edge of the elastic provides a convenient turning guide. Adjust the sewing machine for a wobble stitch with a length of 1.5mm and a width of 1.5mm. Topstitch from the right side of the garment, catching the very edge of the fabric.

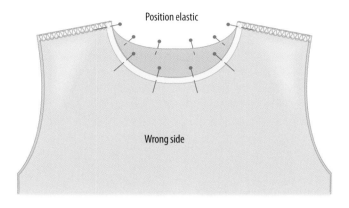

Position elastic

Wrong side

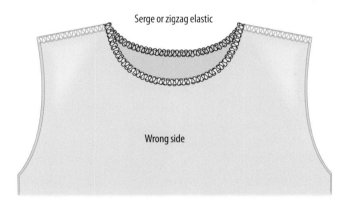

Serge or zigzag elastic

Wrong side

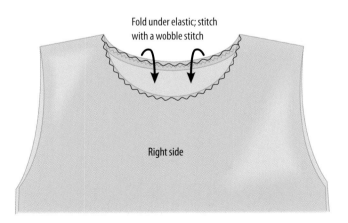

Fold under elastic; stitch with a wobble stitch

Right side

Note from Nancy

As an option to the wobble stitching, insert a double needle and use it to sew the final row of stitching. Two parallel rows of straight stitching will be visible on the right side of the garment, while on the underside a single bobbin thread will zigzag back and forth between the two needle threads.

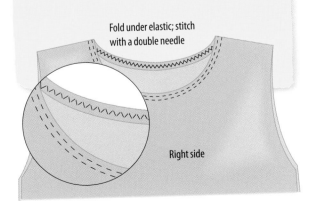

Fold under elastic; stitch with a double needle

Right side

Drawcord elastic

Drawcord elastic is the ideal elastic to apply to the waistline area of lounge pants, sportswear or other casual wear that requires tightening with just a pull on the drawcord. It's prevalently used in ready-to-wear, and because it is knitted, it doesn't lose its integrity or stretch when you stitch through it. Use your serger in tandem with a sewing machine to achieve a clean professional finish to your elastic.

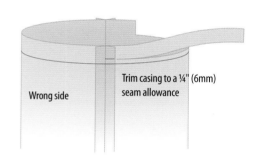

1. Cut and stitch the elastic.

- Cut the elastic 2"–3" (5cm to 8cm) smaller than the waistline measurement.

- Join the short ends of the elastic with a ¼" (6mm) seam allowance. Open seam. If desired, stitch down edges of the seam allowances.

- Join the short ends of the elastic with a ¼" (6mm) seam allowance. Open seam. If desired, stitch down edges of the seam allowances.

- Quarter-mark the elastic with pins or a fabric marking pen, using the seam as one of the quarter marks.

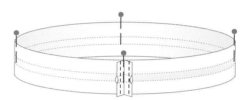

Quarter-mark the elastic

2. Prepare the waistline.

- If the pattern allows a traditional 1¼" (31mm) casing, mark ¼" (6mm) beyond the casing fold. Trim off the excess casing. Only a ¼" (6mm) seam allowance is required for the elastic application.

- Quarter-mark the waistline with pins or a fabric marking pen.

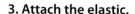

Wrong side

Trim casing to a ¼" (6mm) seam allowance

3. Attach the elastic.

- Join the right side of the elastic to the right side of the garment, positioning the elastic seam at the center back of the waistline.

- Match quartermarks of elastic and garment.

- Serge or zigzag the elastic to the cut edge of the waistline, removing pins as you come to them and stretching elastic to fit.

To use a serger to attach the elastic:

- Use a 4-thread overlock.
- Disengage the blade to prevent nipping the elastic.
- Take two or three stitches to secure the threads before beginning to stretch the elastic. Stitch upper edge of elastic to the garment.

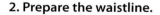

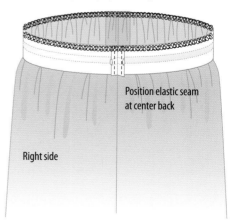

Serge or zigzag elastic to garment

Position elastic seam at center back

Right side

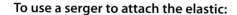

To use a sewing machine to attach the elastic:

- Insert a ballpoint needle.
- Adjust the sewing machine for a zigzag. If your machine has a free arm, position the waistline over the free arm for ease of stitching. Take two or three stitches to secure the threads.
- Stitch along the upper edge of the elastic, starting at the center front and stretching the elastic to fit the waistline.

4. Fold the elastic to the wrong side. Pin at side and center seams at each quarter mark. Using a sewing machine, stitch lower edge of elastic to garment, stretching the elastic to fit.

5. Pull up the cord through the middle of the elastic at the center front.

6. Clip the cords and knot the end of each cord. Optional: Apply seam sealant to the cord ends.

7. When wearing the garment, pull up the cords to fit. Tie ends for a comfy, adjustable waistline finish.

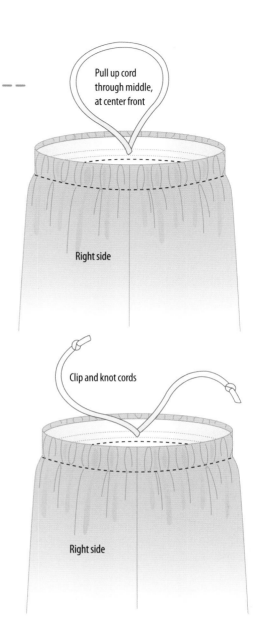

Pull up cord through middle, at center front

Right side

Clip and knot cords

Right side

Pull and tie ends to fit

Fold-over elastic

Fold-over elastic creates a soft flexible finish on knits such as baby clothes and fleece. One side has a plush finish; it's super-soft next to the skin. There's no need to finish the edge of the 62% nylon/28% polyester/10% spandex elastic. Just fold the elastic on its center line and stitch in place. The white fold-over elastic can be dyed to match your fabric.

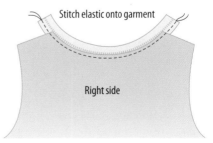

Wrong side is shinier and rougher

Right side is softer

1. Examine the elastic.

- Elastic is 1" (25mm) wide with a foldline. Finished folded width will be ½" (13mm).
- One side of the elastic is softer than the other. Use the soft side as the outside, with the shinier and rougher side toward the inside.
- Outer edges of the elastic are knitted; the center is not. This allows the elastic to easily fold in half.

2. Trim off outer seam allowances from the fabric, if applicable.

3. Align the rougher wrong side of the elastic to the wrong side of the fabric, placing the fabric cut edge at the base of the elastic fold. Don't cut the elastic to size until you're finished with the first stitching.

4. Apply the elastic, using a two-step method.

- Stitch a presser foot width from the fabric edge. It may be necessary to hold the fabric at a slight tension, especially around curves, so the finished edge hugs the body.
- Fold the elastic to the right side. Insert a stretch needle and edgestitch as close to the edge as possible. It should not be necessary to stretch the edge; it will feed almost automatically.
- Cut off excess elastic after stitching.

Note from Nancy

It is easier and more accurate to stitch the folded elastic from the fabric side. Double-check that the stitching catches the elastic.

Trim off seam allowance

Align rougher side of elastic to wrong side of fabric

Right side

Stitch elastic onto garment

Right side

Fold elastic to right side; stitch

Right side

Note from Nancy

This elastic can be dyed to match another fabric. Follow the instructions that come with the elastic and use a generic dyeing method. The plush side will accept the dye more readily than the wrong side, again helping distinguish right from wrong sides.

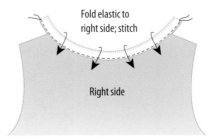

Wrong side colors lighter

Right side colors darker

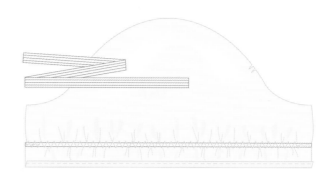

Baby elastic

In lieu of using a fabric casing for elastic, a casing can be created with thread for narrow elastic on children's garments. It's an extremely fast technique and a great elastic option!

1. Select ⅛"–¼" (3mm to 6mm) packaged elastic, or choose a wider knitted elastic that can be trimmed to the desired size by cutting along the ribs of the elastic.

2. Cut the elastic to the length indicated on the pattern plus the width of the seam allowances.

3. Whenever possible, use the flat construction method, applying the elastic to flat garment sections before seaming them together. Work on a flat surface; mark the casing/stitching line on the wrong side of the fabric with a washable marking pen.

4. Couch the elastic to the garment.

- Place the end of the elastic at one edge of the marked casing. Straight stitch two to four stitches and backstitch to secure the elastic.

- Adjust the sewing machine for a zigzag, using a stitch length of 2.5mm and a width that will encase, but not stitch through, the elastic. Test stitching on a fabric remnant before stitching on the garment to ensure you won't stitch through the elastic, or the elastic will not stretch.

- Stretch elastic as you sew, positioning the elastic along the marked casing/stitching line. Stretch the elastic so the marking on the elastic aligns with the cut edge of the seam. Zigzag elastic to the garment.

- At the end of the stitching, change to a straight stitch for several stitches to anchor the stitching and secure the elastic. If elastic was not precut, trim elastic to marked size.

5. Stitch garment seams, securing the elastic in the seamline.

Note from Nancy

I often prefer to mark the length of the elastic right on the elastic rather than cutting the elastic to size before I apply it. That gives me better control while I'm applying the elastic, and I can easily cut the elastic to size after I complete the stitching.

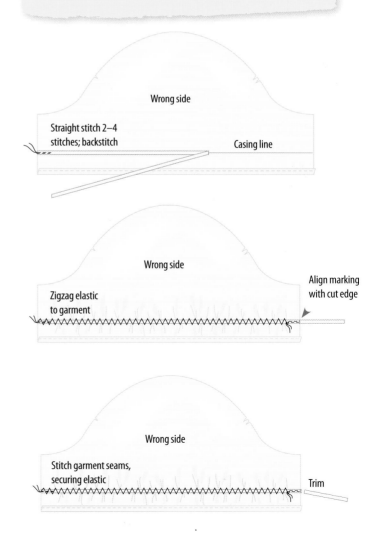

Wrong side

Straight stitch 2–4 stitches; backstitch

Casing line

Wrong side

Zigzag elastic to garment

Align marking with cut edge

Wrong side

Stitch garment seams, securing elastic

Trim

Fantastic Elastic casing technique

Use Fantastic Elastic (page 28) for this casing technique borrowed from ready-to-wear. This elastic can be trimmed to just about any size by simply cutting along a rib, and it won't ravel like braided or woven elastic. The waistline has a drapeable look, with no stitching on the right side as in other casings. Use this technique on skirts or pants.

1. Cut and stitch the elastic.

- Cut the elastic to the desired width, cutting within one of the ribs on the elastic.
- Cut the elastic to the desired length, measuring snuggly around the waistline and cutting the elastic 2"–3" (5cm to 8cm) shorter than that measurement.
- Cut a 2" (5cm) square of firmly woven fabric. Kiss both short ends of the elastic to the fabric and zigzag, taking care to avoid twisting the elastic.
- Trim off the excess fabric square.

2. Stitch or serge the side and center seams of the garment.

3. Quarter-mark the elastic and the waistline on the garment.

4. Align the right side of the elastic to the wrong side of the garment, matching and pinning the quartermarks.

5. Sew or serge the elastic to the top edge of the waistline, stretching the elastic to fit the fabric.

Cut elastic to size along a rib

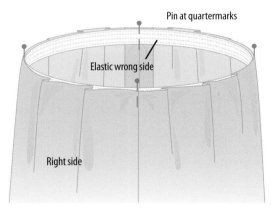

"Kiss" and zigzag elastic ends on fabric square

Pin at quartermarks

Elastic wrong side

Right side

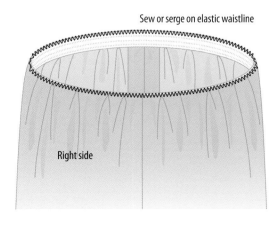

Sew or serge on elastic waistline

Right side

6. Fold the elastic to the inside of the garment, aligning seams. Pin at side and center seams, pinning from the right side.

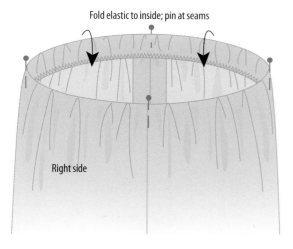

Fold elastic to inside; pin at seams

Right side

7. Stitch in the ditch, straight stitching through the side and center seams to hold the casing in place.

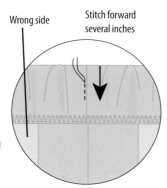

Wrong side

Stitch forward several inches

- Begin sewing about ¼" (6mm) from the upper edge, stitching forward for several stitches.

- Reverse stitching, sewing back to the casing fold.

- Stitch forward again to the end of the elastic. Lock stitches.

- Repeat at each of the garment seams to hold the elastic in position.

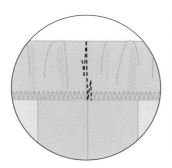

Note from Nancy

If you are making leggings, use this technique for a flawless fit at the waist and crotch:

1. When cutting out your pattern, add several inches (centimeters) to the top of the waistline to allow for the casing.

2. Stitch the inseams and crotch of the leggings.

3. Try on the leggings, wrong side out.

4. Place the waistline elastic at the natural waistline over the top of the leggings.

5. Mark the waistline along the upper edge of the elastic.

6. Remove the leggings and the elastic, and turn the leggings right side out. Join the elastic ends.

7. Quarter-mark the waistline of the leggings and the elastic.

8. Pin the elastic to the wrong side of the waistline, matching the quartermarks with the lower edge of the elastic along the marked line.

9. Stitch along the upper edge of the elastic with an overlock or zigzag stitch, stretching the elastic to fit the waistline. If you have used a zigzag stitch, trim the excess fabric above the elastic. If you used a serger, it trims as it stitches.

10. Fold the elastic to the wrong side of the waistline, encasing it.

11. Stitch through all layers at the lower edge of the elastic, using a wide zigzag or a multi-zigzag stitch.

Mark waistline along upper edge of elastic

Wrong side

5

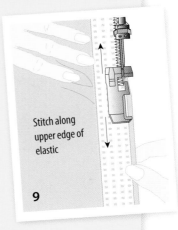

Stitch along upper edge of elastic

9

11

Stitch through all layers

Picot edge elastic

Picot elastic gives a lacy look on lingerie and on your favorite neckline.

1. Use picot elastic for a neckline finish. Select matching or coordinating picot edge lingerie elastic in ⅜" (10mm) or ½" (13mm) width.

2. Overlap front and back patterns at the shoulder. Measure the seamline (not the cutting line) of the pattern neckline or armhole opening. Double that measurement, since the patterns are only half the completed garment. Add ½" (13mm) for joining the elastic.

3. Join the elastic into a circle with a ¼" (6mm) seam; finger press the seam open.

4. Quarter-mark the elastic with pins.

5. Pin the elastic to the opening, right sides together; with the straight edge of the elastic even with the fabric edge. Match quartermarks.

6. Stitch close to, but not into, the picot edge with a narrow to medium zigzag stitch. No stretching is necessary, since the zigzag has built-in stretch.

7. Trim the fabric under the elastic close to the stitching. (This may not be necessary if the elastic is less than ½" (13mm) wide.)

8. Turn the elastic to the wrong side, exposing the picot edge.

9. Zigzag the elastic to the neckline, stitching next to the fold on the right side of the garment, just below the picot edge. Use a slightly longer and wider stitch so you don't build up stitches.

Note from Nancy

Since the elastic is applied to the garment in a 1:1 ratio, it may seem unnecessary to quarter the elastic and fabric to match those quartermarks. But sometimes the fabric stretches slightly as you apply the elastic. Matching those quarter points ensures that each portion of the opening will retain its original shape.

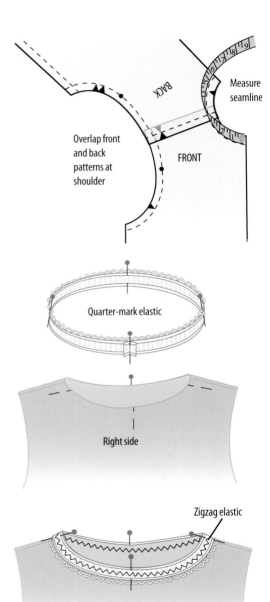

Measure seamline

Overlap front and back patterns at shoulder

BACK

FRONT

Quarter-mark elastic

Right side

Zigzag elastic

Right side

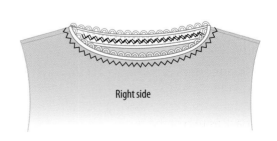

Right side

Necklines

Use ribbing, a facing, a raw edge, a knit trim edge, or one of the new novelty trimmed edges on your knit neckline. They're all easy to sew and they're a made-in-heaven match for a knit top or dress.

Ribbing or self-fabric

Necklines, cuffs and waistlines of knit garments are often finished with knit banding. Banding must fit snugly, and yet be able to stretch so it slips easily over the body. Use traditional ribbing, which resembles a purl/knit construction and has considerable stretch, or a knit fabric with a minimum of 50% stretch.

1. Determine the banding size.

- Patterns often indicate the length of the banding. However, you can determine an appropriate size by overlapping front and back patterns at the shoulder seam and measuring the neckline seamline. Use ¾ of that measurement.
- Bend the folded end of the tape measure over to meet the finished end of the tape measure. The number at the new fold is the length to cut the banding.
- Optional: Add ½" (13mm) for seam allowances. Often this is not necessary, since the stretch of the banding is sufficient to accommodate the extra ½" (13mm).
- Banding widths vary, depending on the style of the shirt. Traditional banding width for an adult's garment is 3½" (9cm), with a 1½" (38mm) finished width. Traditional banding width for a child's garment is 2½" (6cm), with a 1" (25mm) finished width.

2. Attach the band to the neckline.

- Stitch the shoulder seams and quarter-mark the neckline.
- Join the short ends of the band with a ¼" (6mm) seam, right sides together. Sew with a conventional sewing machine, as it is much less bulky.
- Finger press the seam open. Pressing with an iron could flatten and remove the stretch from the band.
- Fold the band in half lengthwise, wrong sides together, meeting cut edges. Optional: Zigzag or straight stitch the edges together to hold the edges in correct position.
- Quarter-mark the band with pins, using the seam as one of the quartermarks.
- Quarter-mark the neckline with pins, using center front and center back as two of the quartermarks.
- Position neckband seam at the center back of the neckline. It will not only look better, but you will always be able to tell the shirt front from the back.

Note from Nancy

It's important that you measure the stitching line, not the cutting line. It's easy to measure the curved neckline if you stand the tape measure on its edge. Since the paper pattern is only half the garment, quickly double that figure by folding the tape measure at the number indicating the half measurement, with the right side of the tape measure visible. The number exposed at the end of the measure is the total length of the neckline. Determine how long to cut the banding as detailed below.

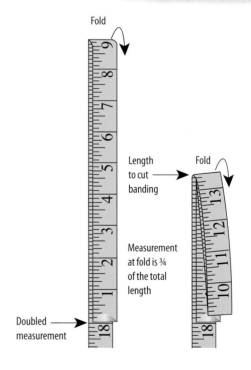

Fold

Length to cut banding

Measurement at fold is ¾ of the total length

Doubled measurement

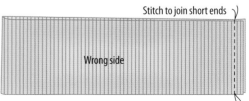

Stitch to join short ends

Wrong side

- Meet quartermarks of neckline and band, right sides together. Pin.
- Stitch or serge the band to the neckline using a ¼" (6mm) allowance.
- If using a sewing machine, straight stitch the band to the garment. Then stitch again using a narrow zigzag.
- If the pattern allows ⅝" (16mm) seams, stitch on the ⅝" (16mm) line. Then trim the seam to ¼" (6mm).
- Topstitch around the neckline with a 4.0 stretch double needle, stitching with the right needle next to the seam and the left needle on the garment. (Some stretch double needles have a blue bar at the top of the two needles, distinguishing them from conventional double needles that may have a red bar.)

3. Optional: Add a double ribbing.

- Cut a second ribbing of a contrasting or coordinating color ½" (13mm) narrower than the initial piece.
- Stitch each ribbing into a circle, right sides together, joining narrow ends.
- Meet the lengthwise edges of each band.
- Stack the narrower band on top of the wider section.
- Zigzag or straight stitch the four edges together so the two bands remain properly positioned.
- Treat the stacked ribbing as one piece and attach the band to the neckline as detailed above with the narrower ribbing meeting the right side of the garment.

4. Here are additional options for decorative neckline trims:

- Finish the neckline with self-fabric with at least 50% stretch. See page 53. (Note: When using self-fabric, cut the fabric on the crosswise grain.)

- Accent the neckline by stitching a row of ½" (13mm) wide or narrower bias tape, braid or other decorative trim around the neckline seam.

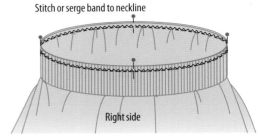

Stitch or serge band to neckline

Right side

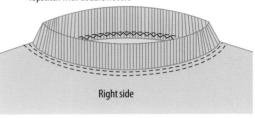

Topstitch with double needle

Right side

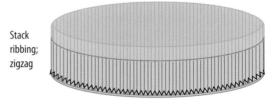

Stack ribbing; zigzag

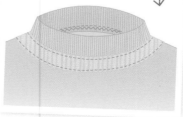

Note from Nancy

Caution: Adding this row of trim reduces the neckline stretch. Be sure the neckline is cut large enough to allow you to easily slip the top over your head.

Recycle ribbing

Here's a ribbing makeover tip: Use the ribbing from the top of socks that have otherwise worn out when making kids' pajamas. The sock ribbing works well on the sleeves and pant legs of pajamas.

Sock top

Serger neckline ribbing (flat method)

This is definitely the easiest method of applying ribbing with a serger. It can be used for cuffs and bottom bands as well as necklines, as shown.

1. Attach the neckline ribbing.

- Stitch only one of the shoulder seams. Quarter-mark the neckline.
- Quarter, but do not seam the ribbing.
- Pin the shirt and ribbing right sides together, matching quartermarks.
- Stretch the ribbing to meet the neckline.
- Serge the ribbing to the neckline with the ribbing on the top. Be careful to match cut edges of ribbing to the unsewn shoulder seam. Don't forget to remove pins as you get to them.

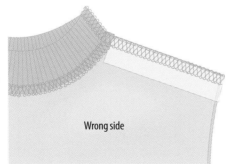

Right side

2. Serge the remaining ribbing and shoulder seam, right sides together, stabilizing the shoulder seam if desired. The ribbing ends should match at the neckline edge.

Wrong side

Facing

A traditional facing is a great finishing option for a knit neckline when you don't care for the look of ribbing. It may be necessary to make the neckline larger. Use the same fabric as the top, or use a cotton print or solid fabric for the facing.

1. Make the pattern.

- Trace the neckline and shoulder seam on the front and back pattern pieces onto pattern paper to use when modifying the pattern, to preserve your original pattern.
- Draw a new neckline on the traced front pattern piece. Start by drawing the neckline ¼" (6mm) below the original neckline at the center front, and tapering to the shoulder seams.
- Cut out the traced front and back pattern pieces. Pin shoulder seams together. Try on the pattern. Make sure that you can get the pattern over your head, especially if you are using a cotton fabric for the facing. If not, you may need to redraw the front neckline a little lower.
- Trace the new neckline for the front and back pieces on pattern paper, adding neckline and shoulder seams.
- Make the new facing about 2¼" (6cm) wide.

2¼" (6cm)

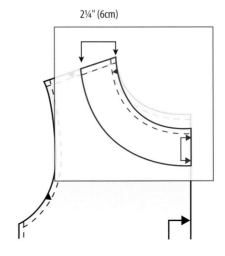

2. Complete facings and stitch to the top.

- Stitch shoulder seams of the top, right sides together. Also stitch shoulder seams of the facings, right sides together.

Wrong side

- Optional: Cut fusible interfacing for facings using the same patterns as the facings. Fuse interfacing to wrong sides of facings before stitching seams.
- Turn up a ¼" (6mm) hem on the facing and topstitch, or simply serge the hem edge.

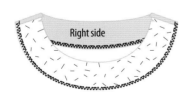

Right side

- Pin and stitch facings to the garment, right sides together, matching shoulder seams, center front, and center back. Press seam open and then toward the facing.

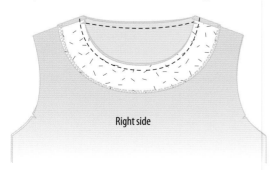

Right side

Note from Nancy

If T-shirt seams are sewn conventionally, grade the facing seam allowances, trimming them slightly narrower than the seams on the T-shirt. If seams are serged, alternate seam directions at the seam intersections.

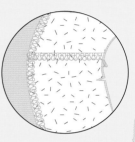

- Understitch the facing, catching the seam to the facing with a multi-zigzag stitch. This prevents the facing from rolling to the right side. Press facing to inside of garment.

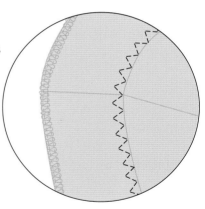

- Optional: Topstitch close to the edge of the neckline or close to the edge of the facing.

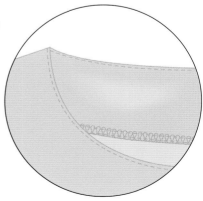

Knit trim edge

Give your knit top an easy, yet fashionable neckline with an "upcycled" look.

1. Prepare the trim and the neckline.

- Measure neckline after the shoulder seams of the knit top have been sewn.
- Add 1½" (4cm) to the neckline measurement to allow for the diagonal seam on the trim. (Example: If your neckline measures 32" [81cm] + 1½" [4cm] = 33½" [85cm].)
- Cut a 1½" (4cm) (wide) × 33½" (85cm) (neckline measurement plus 1½" [4cm] length) crosswise strip of knit fabric with at least 25% stretch.
- Join the ends diagonally, right sides together. Trim the seam to ¼" (6mm).

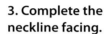

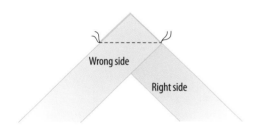

2. Attach trim to neckline.

- Quarter the neckline and knit trim. Pin mark.

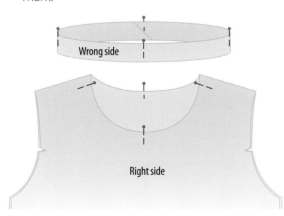

- Match quartermarks, right sides together, and stitch with a ¼" (6mm) seam, matching cut edges of neckline and knit trim. Stretch knit trim slightly around the curved edge.

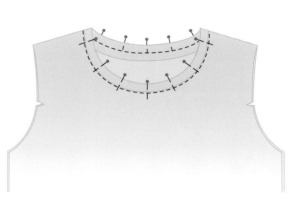

3. Complete the neckline facing.

- Press the trim to the wrong side of the T-shirt, with approximately ¼" (6mm) of trim showing on the right side of the garment; pin in place.
- Stitch in the ditch of the seam.
- Trim the excess knit trim close to stitching on the wrong side of the neckline.

Note from Nancy

Use appliqué scissors with a pelican bill on the underside of the seam allowance when trimming the neck edge. The beveled edge prevents you from cutting into the top as you trim the seam close to the stitching.

Serge 'n go finish

Here's a fast and easy way to finish the neckline or edges of slinky and other knits. Serging adds a subtle and decorative touch as it cascades down the front of a jacket. Simple serging with decorative threads is all that's required.

1. Set up the serger.

- Thread both loopers with decorative thread. Try combining a heavier weight variegated cotton thread with a solid-colored rayon thread; the addition of the rayon thread adds an interesting highlight. Stack the two threads and thread them through the serger as if they were a single thread.
- Match the needle thread to the fabric.
- Adjust the machine for a 3-thread overlock. Remove the right needle; use only the left needle.
- Set stitch length at 2mm–3mm.

2. Determine where to guide the fabric edge.

- Trim away the entire ⅝" (16mm) seam allowance as you serge.
- Measure ⅝" (16mm) from the inside of the blade to determine where to position the edge of the fabric. If your machine has markings to indicate the stitching position, follow the appropriate marking. If there are no markings, add a piece of tape to identify where to guide the fabric edge.

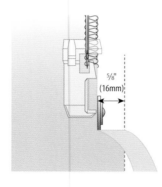

3. Serge along the edge.

- Raise the presser foot, align the fabric edge with the marked position, lower the presser bar and serge one edge, leaving a thread tail.
- Take your time! You want the serging to be straight, not wobbly.

Note from Nancy

Test serging on fabric scraps to ensure you have sufficient coverage along the edge so it looks like a trim. If serging appears too tight or too loose, adjust settings and test again.

- Serge the adjacent edge. Raise the toe of the presser foot; position the fabric, and serge, trimming off the first thread tail. Again leave a thread tail at the end of the serging.

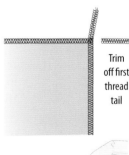

Trim off first thread tail

- Place a drop of seam sealant such as Fray Check at the corners; let it dry.

- Thread the serger tail into a double eyed needle and weave the thread tail into the existing serger stitches.

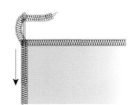

Turn 'n stitch finish

The way in which you finish neckline edges depends on both the fabric you select and the pattern style. This technique is ideal for fabrics such as slinky knits, when a minimal finish is all that's required.

1. Seam the garment using a size 75 stretch or ballpoint needle. Thread the needle and bobbin with all-purpose polyester thread. Serge seams or use a wobble stitch as detailed on page 36.

2. Staystitch the neckline on the seamline in any areas that contain points or corners. Fusible interfacing strips may also be added to these areas for reinforcement.

3. Clip to staystitching on inner corners. Be careful not to cut the stitching.

4. Serge along the outer edge with a 3- or 4-thread overlock, trimming off excess seam allowances so ¼" (6mm) remains. This line of serging adds some support to the edge.

5. Turn under the seam allowance, following the serged stitching.

6. Topstitch along the edge using two rows of machine stitching. Or, use a 3mm or 4mm ballpoint double needle and all-purpose cotton thread.

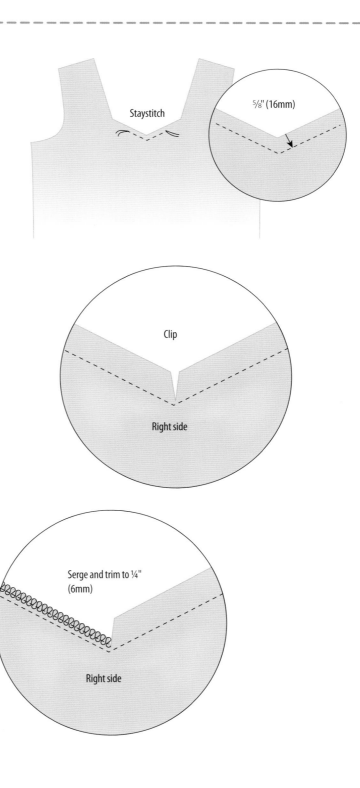

Staystitch

⅝" (16mm)

Clip

Right side

Serge and trim to ¼" (6mm)

Right side

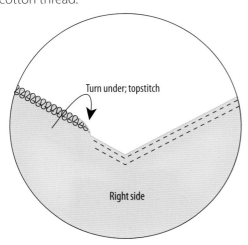

Turn under; topstitch

Right side

Pockets

I've included my favorite inseam pocket and a child's patch pocket with rib trim. Both techniques require some minor pattern modifications, but they are decidedly easy for knits!

All-in-one side pockets

Traditional side pocket applications require four seams, which sometimes add bulk. Here's a way to save time and eliminate much of the bulk: Combine pattern pieces before doing any cutting.

1. Make a duplicate of the pocket pattern, transferring all markings. Be sure to mark the dots where the side seam should end at the top and bottom of the pocket. (Using a photocopier is a quick and easy way to make the duplicate pattern.)

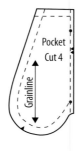

2. Place the original pocket pattern on the garment front pattern, aligning markings and stitching lines. Pin or tape the two pattern pieces together. Repeat on the garment back.

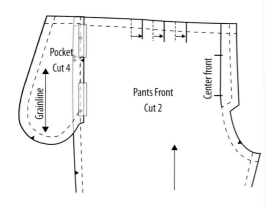

Note from Nancy

Using this timesaving technique sometimes requires additional yardage because the modified pattern pieces are wider than the original patterns. Before cutting out the patterns, check that you have adequate yardage. If you modify the patterns before purchasing fabric, do a rough layout to ensure you purchase the correct amount of fabric.

3. Cut out the garment, using the modified front and back patterns.

4. Transfer pattern markings.

5. Stitch and complete the pocket.

- Meet the right sides of the garment front and back. Stitch the side seam from the hem edge to the dot marking the lower edge of the pocket opening. Pivot and continue stitching around the pocket to the waistline edge.

- Stitch the side seam from the upper pocket opening to the waistline. To reinforce this stitching, add a second line of stitching over the first.

- On the back garment sections, clip the seam allowance to the pivot point. Press the seam open, pressing the pocket toward the front.

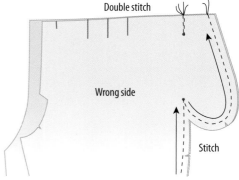

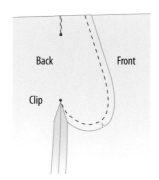

Rib trim gathered pocket

A simple rib trim gathered pocket is a super option to use on children's clothes. The pocket is snug at the top yet fits lots of child-size trinkets.

1. Trace a regular patch pocket pattern, sized for the garment you are making.

2. Cut ribbing 2" (5cm) wide by the length of the pocket top measurement.

3. Prepare pocket for gathers.

- Trim ¾" (19mm) off the top of the pocket pattern.
- Mark vertical lines ½"–1" (13mm to 25mm) apart on the pocket.
- Cut on the marked lines, but not through the bottom edge of the pocket.
- Spread the pocket open at the slashes and tape to the pattern paper. Trace.

4. Prepare pocket for ribbing.

- Cut the new pattern from the fabric.
- Turn under the bottom edges of the pocket on the seamline and press.
- Fold the ribbing in half, right sides together, and stitch the short edges.
- Turn the ribbing right side out.
- Place the raw edges of the ribbing on top of the raw edge of the pocket and stitch or serge with a ¼" (6mm) seam.
- Press the ribbing toward the pocket.

5. Topstitch the pocket in position on the clothing.

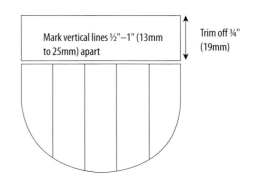

Mark vertical lines ½"–1" (13mm to 25mm) apart

Trim off ¾" (19mm)

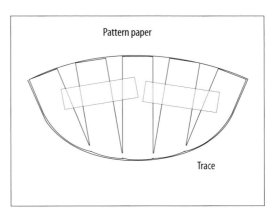

Pattern paper

Trace

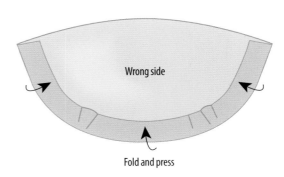

Wrong side

Fold and press

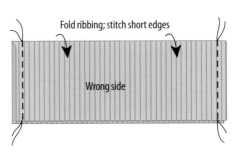

Fold ribbing; stitch short edges

Wrong side

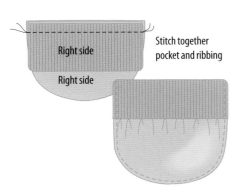

Right side

Right side

Stitch together pocket and ribbing

Buttonholes

Buttonholes are a very functional part of a knit garment. Because a knit stretches, sewists sometimes are hesitant to use buttonholes as closures. No one likes buttonholes that sag or stretch out of shape. Here's how to maintain the original size of the buttonhole. No rippling effect here!

1. Interface the wrong side of the fabric on the area for buttons and buttonholes for added body and support and to minimize stretching. 100% polyester fusible knit interfacing is best because it is very compatible with knit fabrics.

- Cut interfacing the same size as the facing.
- Position the interfacing on the wrong side of the facing. Cover with a damp cloth and press to fuse.
- Attach facing as indicated in the pattern instructions.

Facing wrong side

Damp press cloth

2. Mark the placement for vertical buttonholes, marking the center front and the buttonhole starting position, on the right side of the garment.

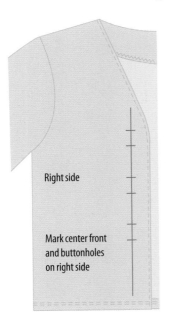

Right side

Mark center front and buttonholes on right side

3. Optional: Stabilize the buttonhole area by covering with a water-soluble stabilizer.

4. Stitch the buttonholes, sewing through the stabilizer, garment, interfacing and facing.

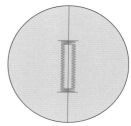

- If the sewing machine has a built-in buttonhole setting for stretch buttonholes, use that setting.

The stitches will not be quite as dense as for buttonholes designed for woven fabrics.

- Loosen the top tension by two numbers or notches.
- Test stitching on a fabric scrap to verify buttonhole length and stitch density.

5. Cut open the buttonholes using a buttonhole cutter set and a two-step process.

- Place the buttonhole on the block so half of the buttonhole extends beyond the block. Place the end of the blade at the end of the buttonhole and cut open that portion of the buttonhole.
- Place the uncut portion of the buttonhole on the block, allowing the cut portion to extend beyond the block. Cut open the remainder of the buttonhole.

6. Trim away excess stabilizer.

> ## Note from Nancy
>
> If your pattern shows horizontal buttonholes, change them to be vertical. Vertical buttonholes are sewn with the stable grain of the knit, while horizontal buttonholes are on the crossgrain, which tends to bow out of shape.

Quick placket

Season-spanning rugby shirts are popular for various sports and casual wear. Making one like this woman's version is easy, especially if you take a few minutes to modify the pattern.

1. Cut and mark the shirt front.

- Place the center front of the shirt on the fabric fold. Cut out the pattern, but not along the placket opening.

- Place a short nip at the center fold at both the neckline and the hemline.

- Mark the center front on the wrong side of the shirt by aligning a ruler between the nips and marking with a fabric pen or pencil.

- Cut a strip of fusible knit interfacing 2" (5cm) wide and 1" (25mm) longer than the front opening.

- Position and fuse the interfacing to the wrong side of the shirt front. Align the right edge at the center front nip.

- Mark the position for the tab front opening ¾" (19mm) to the left of the center front. Draw an opening 6" (15cm) long, parallel to the center front.

2. Make a new facing/placket pattern.

- Place tissue paper over the front pattern piece, extending the paper 1" (25mm) beyond center front. Mark "Place on fold" along the edge of the pattern.
- Outline the neckline cutting line.
- Outline half the shoulder cutting line (about 2½" [6cm]).
- Mark the front placket 7" (18cm) long.
- Draw the lower edge 4½" (11cm) wide.
- Connect the shoulder cutting line to the lower edge with a slight arc.

3. Cut out the new pattern, placing it on the fabric fold. Nip the fold at the neckline and the lower edge. Also, cut the pattern from fusible knit interfacing.

4. Fuse the interfacing to the wrong side of the facing.

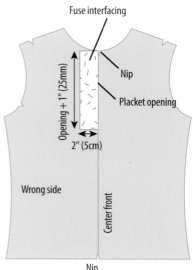

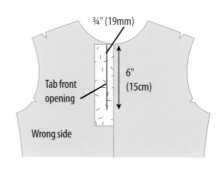

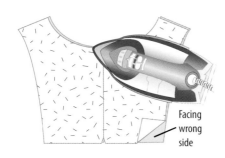

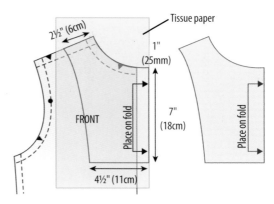

5. Mark the facing/placket.

- Mark the center front on the wrong side of the facing/placket, aligning the nips at the neckline and hemline with a ruler and marking with a fabric pen or pencil.
- Mark the tab opening ¾" (19mm) to the left of the center front. Make the opening 6" (15cm) long and parallel to the center front.

6. Attach the facing/placket to the shirt front.

- Meet the facing/placket to the front, right sides together, matching tab line markings. (Note: When the two tab lines are stacked, shoulder areas will not match.)
- Center ¼" (6mm) wash-away double-sided tape (for stitching) over the marked tab opening. The tape serves as a stitching guide.
- Stitch along the edges of the tape, sewing to a point at the end of the marked opening. Shorten the stitch length on each side of the point to reinforce the seam.
- Remove the tape. Cut along the tab front opening. If desired, restitch the opening for reinforcement.
- Turn the facing/placket to the wrong side; match shoulder seams. On the left side, the two fabrics align at the stitching line. On the right side, a placket extension is formed.

7. Join the front and back at the shoulder

seams, right sides together. Do not catch the placket/facing in the seams.

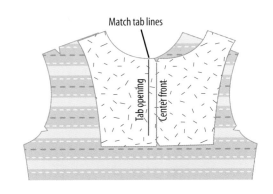

Match tab lines

Tab opening

Center front

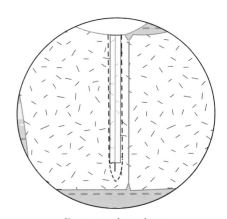

Shorten around tape, shorten stitch length at point

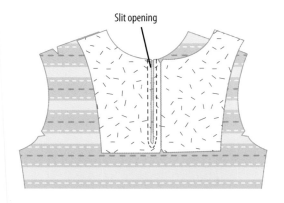

Slit opening

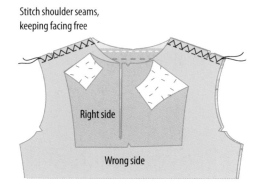

Stitch shoulder seams, keeping facing free

Right side

Wrong side

8. Attach the collar.

- Use a premade knit collar, or create a self-fabric collar if the pattern pieces are included in the pattern.

- Pin the collar to the neckline, meeting the right collar edge to the center front nip of the top and the left collar edge to the nip on the facing/placket.

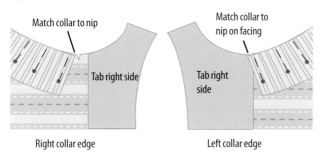

Right collar edge   Left collar edge

- Wrap the facing/placket to the outside, sandwiching the collar in between. Match the right and left shoulder seams of the facing to the shoulder seams of the top. Pin.

- Stitch the neckline.

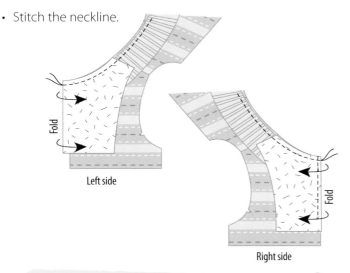

Left side

Right side

Note from Nancy

On the left side, aligning the facing shoulder seam to the top shoulder seam allows the tab to fold back on itself and form a placket. You may need to stretch the facing a bit because it has been stabilized with interfacing.

- Turn the collar and neckline right side out using a point-former/tube-turner tool.

9. Stitch a rectangle across the bottom of the tab opening.

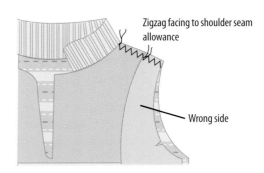

Stitch across bottom of tab opening

10. Stitch the shoulder seams of the facing to the shoulder seam allowances with a narrow zigzag.

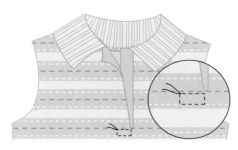

Zigzag facing to shoulder seam allowance

Wrong side

11. Stitch vertical buttonholes or use snap closures.

Hems

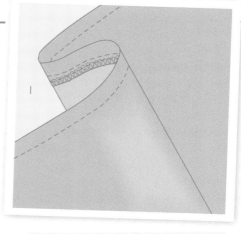

No more hand hemming! The two conventional methods shown here are knit friendly, and hems lie flat and straight. If you own a serger, try one of the serger methods on the following pages. Make sure to check your serger instruction manual to see what capabilities it features for hems. These beguiling hems invite you to enjoy the ease and sensibility of sewing with knits.

Conventional hems

Fuse-pressed and topstitched

The easiest method of hemming is to press and topstitch. What could possibly be easier?

1. Press the hem, using a hem gauge. This allows you to press the hem without having an imprint on the right side of the fabric. With relatively stable knits such as double knits, interlocks or other knits that have weight and substance, that's all the preparation that's needed.

2. For lightweight stretchy knits or those that tend to roll and curl, add a strip of fusible web to the underside of the hem.

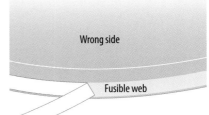

- If using paper-backed fusible web, cut strips ¼"–⅜" (6mm–10mm) wide. Unfold the hem and press the web to the inside of the hem, using plenty of steam. Then remove the paper backing.

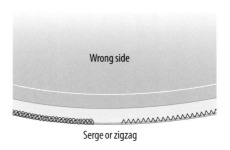

Serge or zigzag

- If using fusible web on a roll, serge or zigzag the web to the inside of the hem. Trim any web that extends beyond the fabric edge so you don't get web on the bottom of the iron when you fuse the hem.
- Fold up the hem; cover with a press cloth and press using plenty of steam. The warmth of the steam allows the fusible web to adhere to the opposite edge, stabilizing it for stitching. Avoid pressing over the hem edge, as this could leave an imprint on the right side of the fabric.

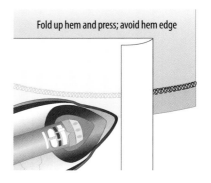

Fold up hem and press; avoid hem edge

3. Topstitch the hem in place using matching thread, slightly increasing stitch length to 3.5mm or 4mm.

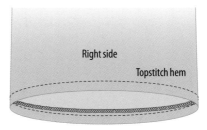

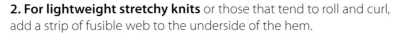

Double-needle hem

A double (twin) needle has two needles attached to a single shaft, so on the right side of a double needle-stitched hem, you'll see two perfectly parallel rows of stitching. On the wrong side, a single bobbin thread moves back and forth between the two needle threads and looks similar to a zigzag. This builds some stretch into the hem as well. Double needle stitching is especially suitable for lightweight or slinky knits.

1. Prepare the hem as for a topstitched hem.

2. Select a double needle. When purchasing double needles, the first number refers to the distance in millimeters between the two needles, while the second number indicates the size of the needle. Use a 3.0/80 or 4.0/80 needle.

3. Use two spools of thread on the top of the machine, positioning them so threads unwind in opposite directions. This prevents the threads from tangling.

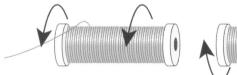

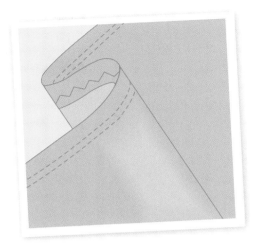

- **Pass the threads through the machine tensions** as if they were a single thread, separating them at the needles.

- **For best results, lengthen the stitch** and slightly loosen the tension. Test stitching on a fabric scrap before stitching on the garment. Adjust tension and stitch length if necessary.

4. Stitch a uniform distance from the hem fold, sewing on the right side of the fabric. Check to ensure stitching catches the hem. Trim excess hem fabric after stitching.

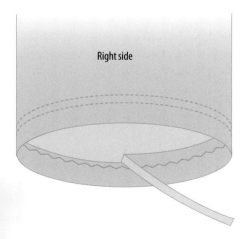

Right side

Serged hems

Serger blind hem

Use a blind hem foot designed for your serger when stitching a blind hem. The blind hem foot allows you to precisely guide the fabric so that rows of flatlocking remain straight.

1. Set up your machine for a flatlock stitch following your instruction manual. It will most likely call for settings similar to these:

- Stitch: 2- or 3-thread flatlock
- Needle: Right
- Width: Normal
- Length: 4mm
- Differential feed: Normal to 1.3
- Blade position: Unlocked (engaged)
- Subsidiary looper: Engaged for 2-thread flatlock only
- Presser foot: Blind hem foot

2. Fold hem to the wrong side of the fabric and pin in place, pinning parallel and close to the fold.

3. Fold the fabric back on itself, leaving at least ¼" (6mm) of the hem extending beyond the fold.

4. Place the fold of the hem under the foot and begin sewing, barely catching the fold with the needle and trimming the extending hem.

5. The adjustable guide to the right of the foot is essential in determining the "bite" of the stitch. Adjust the guide on the foot by loosening the screw and sliding the guide left or right, moving the guide closer to or farther away from the needle. If too much thread shows on the right side of the garment, move the guide farther away from the needle (to the right). If the needle thread doesn't catch the hem, move the guide closer to the needle (to the left).

6. Pull stitches flat and press when hem is complete.

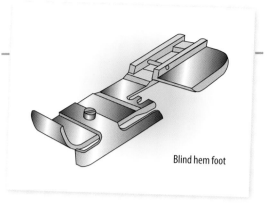

Blind hem foot

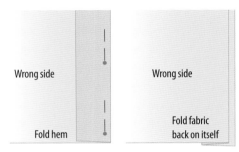

Wrong side

Fold hem

Wrong side

Fold fabric back on itself

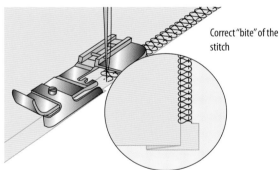

Correct "bite" of the stitch

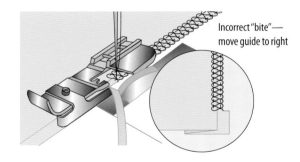

Incorrect "bite"— move guide to right

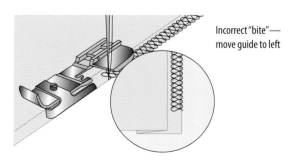

Incorrect "bite"— move guide to left

Cover-stitched hem

Hems on many ready-to-wear garments are commonly finished with a cover stitch. This serger stitch is both functional and decorative. On the right side it simulates double needle stitching, while on the wrong side the threads encase the fabric and resemble an overlock, without trimming away any fabric.

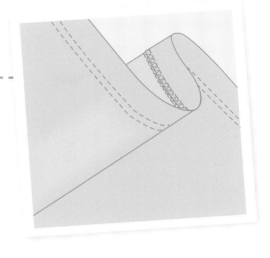

1. Check your owner's manual to see if your serger can stitch a cover stitch. Not all sergers have this capability. Adjust the serger for a cover stitch, following these general guidelines. Refer to your owner's manual for specifics for your machine.

- Disengage the blades. No fabric will be trimmed away.
- Disengage the upper looper.
- Add the flatbed sewing table component to your serger.
- Space the needles at the widest needle positions (left and right needles—not the center needle position).
- Thread the cover stitch looper and the two needles with all-purpose thread matched to the fabric.

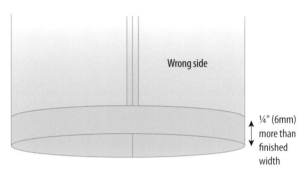

Wrong side

¼" (6mm) more than finished width

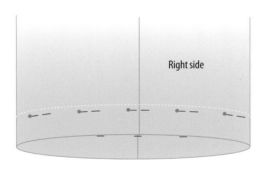

Right side

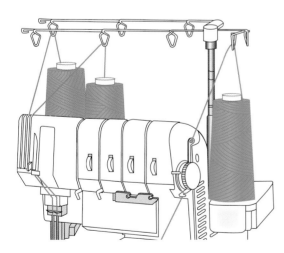

- Add a fabric guide to your serger, if available. It is an excellent guiding tool.
- Do a test stitching. If the fabric puckers, check the differential feed. If necessary, adjust the differential feed and/or stitch length.

2. Press up a hem allowance ¼" (6mm) wider than the finished hem width.

3. Place a mark on the right side of the fabric to indicate the hem position. Pin the hem, placing pins parallel to and about ¼" (6mm) from the cut edge of the hem, with heads facing you.

4. Measure the distance from that mark to the folded edge of the hem. If your machine has markings to indicate stitching positions, guide the fabric along the appropriate marking. If there are no markings, place a piece of tape on the serger to help identify where to guide the fabric.

5. Position the fabric by placing the pins under the center of the presser foot. Remove the pin and serge, guiding the folded fabric edge along the marked guide. Remove all pins as you come to them.

6. End the hemming process by sewing 3–4 stitches on top of the initial cover stitching.

7. Release the thread from the stitch finger.

- Raise both the presser foot and the needles.

- Insert your finger under the thread above the needles; draw up some slack. The stitches will release from the stitch finger. Clip threads, leaving long thread tails.

- Draw the threads to the wrong side. Tie them together or apply seam sealant; then clip the thread tails.

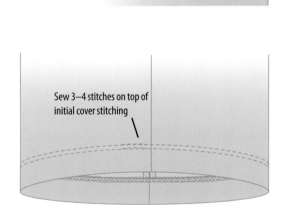

Position pins in center of presser foot

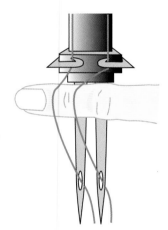

Sew 3–4 stitches on top of initial cover stitching

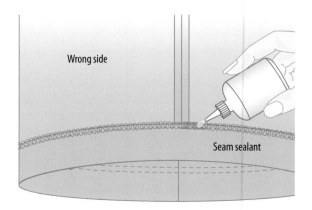

Wrong side

Seam sealant

Zippers

The "dreaded" zipper has just lost its threat! Try one of the following exposed zipper techniques for knits. The separating zipper works well in sportweight knits and polar fleece jackets. Included here are two versions—one with a facing and one with ribbing. An exposed zipper is a major style point on pockets and other areas where you would like a functional embellishment.

Separating zipper in a garment with facing

Use this easy technique to put a zipper in a lightweight jacket, knit top or sweatshirt that includes a facing. Minimal stitching with maximum results!

1. Measure from just below the neckline seam to just above the hemline to determine the zipper length. Adjust the hem width or the distance the zipper is placed above the hemline to determine the exact position for the separating zipper.

2. Attach the zipper foot to your machine, following the manufacturer's instructions.

3. Pin the closed zipper along the left front edge of the garment, right sides together, with the zipper stop just below the seamline at the top of the garment. Fold the excess tape at the upper edge away from the zipper teeth.

4. Stitch up the center of the zipper tape, allowing space for the slider to move; remove pins as you stitch. Trim excess zipper tape that was folded away from the teeth at the top of the zipper.

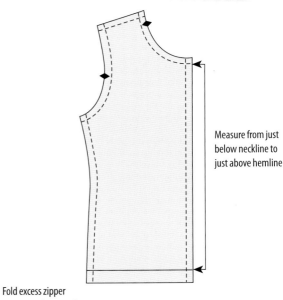

Measure from just below neckline to just above hemline

Fold excess zipper tape away from teeth

Right side

Stitch

Note from Nancy

If your fabric is lightweight, fuse a 1" (25mm) strip of knit interfacing to the wrong side along both center fronts.

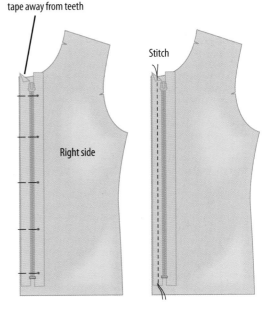

5. Place the zipper and garment left front right side up. Finger press the fabric fold close to the zipper teeth.

6. Mark remaining side of the zipper and right front of the garment in areas critical for matching.

7. Open the zipper and match the remaining zipper edge to the right front garment edge, right sides together. Pin in place, folding the excess tape at the upper edge away from the teeth of the zipper, as before.

8. Stitch down the center of the zipper tape, allowing space for the slider. Trim excess folded zipper tape.

9. Fold the zipper to the wrong side of the fabric, and finger press the fabric fold close to the zipper teeth.

10. Finish facing.

- Stitch facing to neckline, right sides together, following pattern instructions.
- Stitch facing in place over previous stitching on the zipper tape.

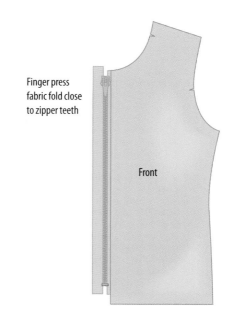

Finger press fabric fold close to zipper teeth

Front

Stitch down center of zipper

Fold zipper to wrong side

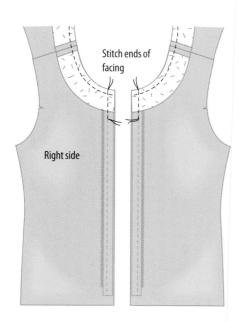

Stitch ends of facing

Right side

- Trim facing corners close to stitching, and turn facing toward the wrong side of the garment.

11. Finish hem.

- Clean finish hem edge by serging, zigzagging, or turning under the hem edge and straight stitching.
- Turn hem to the right side of the garment over zipper tape.
- Stitch hem to zipper following previous stitching line. Trim hem corner.
- Turn hem toward wrong side of the garment and stitch in place.

12. On the right side of the garment, topstitch ¼" (6mm) from the fold on each side of the zipper.

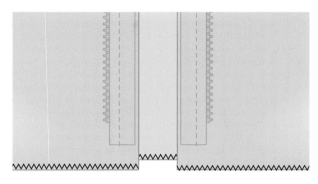

Clean finish hem edge

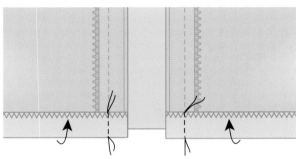

Stitch hem to zipper

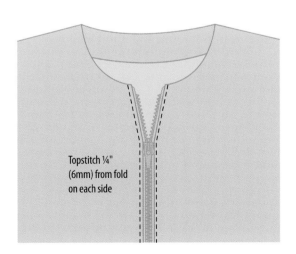

Topstitch ¼" (6mm) from fold on each side

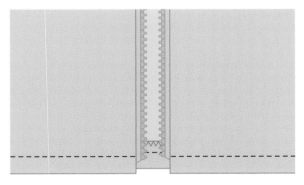

Turn hem toward wrong side; stitch

Separating zipper in a ribbed garment

Easily place a zipper in a jacket, knit top, or sweatshirt pattern that includes ribbing at the neckline and possibly the hemline.

1. Follow the pattern to complete the shoulder seams, sleeves, and hem or bottom ribbing (if applicable). Neckline ribbing is added later.

2. Prepare the zipper.

- Mark the right (R) and left (L) sides of the zipper and center front of the garment (as you would wear it), using a water-erasable marking pen.
- Check the length of the zipper.

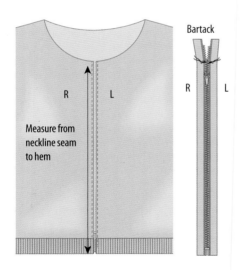

(1) Measure from base of hem or bottom ribbing to the neckline seam. The zipper should extend beyond the neckline seam.

(2) Bartack the zipper tape, at the measured length, just above the last zipper tooth on each side, so that you don't accidently zip off the zipper pull as you are working on the zipper.

(3) Remove excess zipper teeth above the bartacks with pliers.

3. Insert the zipper.

- Mark a horizontal line across the zipper on the wrong side, to use for matching the zipper edges as they are sewn to the center front.
- Align wash-away double-sided tape (for stitching) along the center front edges, on the right side of garment. Remove the paper backing from the tape.
- Unzip the zipper and align the right side of the zipper to the right side of the garment, with zipper tape and center front edges even. Repeat for the left side, lining up the neckline edges, as well as the horizontal line on the zipper.
- Attach the zipper foot to your sewing machine following directions in your manual.
- Stitch the zipper to both sides of the garment close to the teeth of the zipper.

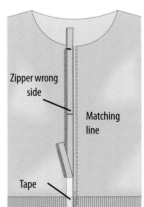

4. Finish the neckline before topstitching the zipper.

- Trim zipper tape even with the top edge of the neckline.
- Add neckline ribbing, aligning the raw edges of the ribbing with the neckline edge. Follow the pattern instructions for stitching.

5. Topstitch.

- Press the zipper tape toward the wrong side of the garment. Pin in place.
- Topstitch about ¼" (6mm) along the center front, catching the zipper in position. Pivot at the neckline seam and continue by stitching in the ditch, catching the ribbing seam on the wrong side.

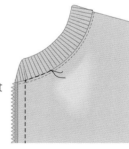

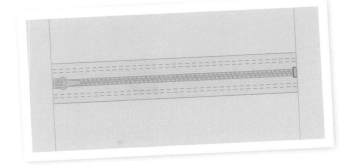

Exposed zipper

The exposed zipper is easy to insert, and it is especially useful as a decorative accent on knits.

1. If necessary, finish the seam edges by serging or zigzagging to prevent raveling.

2. Position a zipper that is 2" (5cm) longer than the pattern recommends along one finished edge, meeting the wrong side of the zipper to the right side of the fabric. Make sure that the fabric is a scant ¼" (6mm) away from the zipper teeth to allow room for opening and closing the zipper. Stitch.

3. Add a second line of stitching close to the first stitching to reinforce the zipper.

4. Repeat, stitching the zipper to the opposite edge of the fabric as detailed above.

Stitch first line

Right side

Stitch second line

Right side

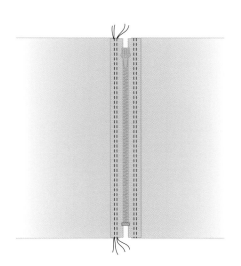

Note from Nancy

Try using this technique with ribbon. Topstitch pieces of grosgrain ribbon to each short edge of the zipper tape. Then stitch strips of ribbon to each long edge of the zipper tape, tucking under the short edges. Center zipper over nonraveling fabric and topstitch ribbon edges to the fabric. Trim excess fabric from the reverse side, exposing the zipper.

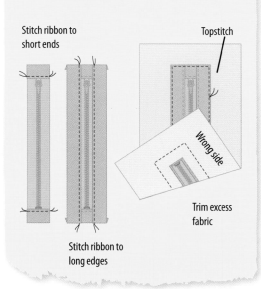

Stitch ribbon to short ends

Topstitch

Wrong side

Trim excess fabric

Stitch ribbon to long edges

Chapter 4

Creative Accents for Knits

New styles and new fabrics have sent those who sew clamoring for updated accent and embellishment techniques shown in ready-to-wear. In this section are some traditional knit embellishments plus lots of fun and speedy accents for a new knit era and a totally flattering style.

Finishing touches

Finishing the edges of knits can definitely be more creative than finishing wovens, mainly because the fabric doesn't ravel. Many knit fashion designers are using a "less is best" approach and leaving the edges of their designs raw, while others are accenting with ruffles, flounces and creative stitching. Knit edges are demure one minute and wild the next. Let's explore some options—both new and updated.

Easy raw-edge finishes

Single, jersey and slinky knits are easy to seam, yet when it comes time to do the hemming step, the lightweight fabric tends to slip and slide. Combine fusible web and an additional fabric—a complementary knit—for an easy finish that trims at the same time. Choose one of the following options.

Option 1: Prevent hems from rolling to the right side on single, jersey and slinky knits.

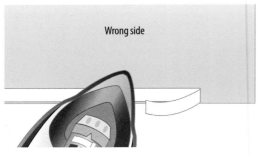

Wrong side

Right side

- Fuse a narrow strip (½" [13mm] wide) of paper-backed fusible web, along the wrong side and top edge of the hem area.

- Remove the paper backing and press up the hem allowance. The fusible strip will prevent the fabric from rolling.

Wrong side

Option 2: Prepare and attach a bias edging.

- Cut bias strips of a complementary knit fabric, ½" (13mm) wider than the hem allowance.

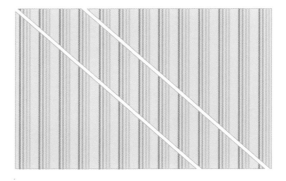

- Join the trim pieces using an overlapped fusible web seam. Press paper-backed fusible web to one trim piece, remove the paper, overlap second the trim section and press. The bias-cut fabrics will not ravel.

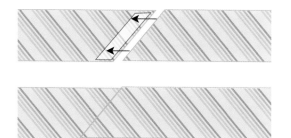

- Overlap the fused hemline onto the trim piece, allowing a ½"–¾" (13mm to 19mm) extension of the trim fabric.

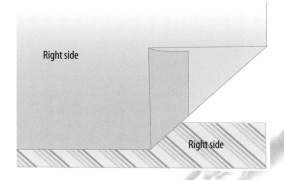

Right side

Right side

- Zigzag or straight stitch all layers from the wrong side, guiding the presser foot along the cut edge. Use a 2mm–2.5mm stitch width and a 2mm stitch length.

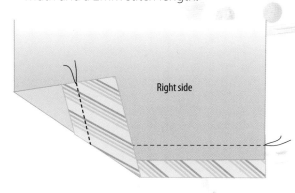

Right side

Note from Nancy

Make a classy version of this knit top with a finished accent. Use 1¾" (4cm) bias-cut nylon organza strips finished with a 3-thread serger rolled edge. Check your serger owner's manual for this elegant stitch. Use rayon embroidery thread in the needle and loopers for an edge with a sheen.

Lettuce edging

Lettuce edging gets its name from the curly edge on ribbing. It is an especially decorative edge for little girls' or feminine necklines, sleeve ribbing and hem ribbing, but it is also suitable for use on interlock knits or swimwear (spandex) knits for a frilly touch. It is easy to accomplish with either a sewing machine or a serger.

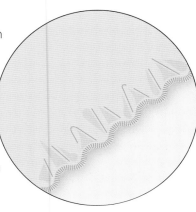

Sewing machine lettuce edge

1. Use a satin stitch on a sewing machine with a narrow zigzag for the width and approximately a 1mm stitch length.

2. Stretch the knit in front of and in back of the presser foot as you are stitching.

3. Make sure the needle stitches over the edge of the fabric on the right swing of the needle.

4. Gently stretch the edge after stitching to increase the lettuce effect.

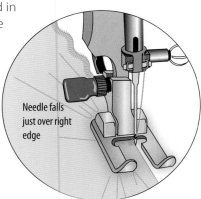

Needle falls just over right edge

Serger lettuce edge

1. Set up your serger for a narrow rolled edge, referring to your instruction manual. Use a normal width and a rolled hem length setting of 1–2.

2. Use woolly nylon thread in the loopers and regular cone thread in the needle for an attractive lettuce edge.

3. Lock or disengage the cutting blade, if possible.

4. Guide the fabric along the right edge of the presser foot.

Stretch

5. Stretch the ribbing an equal amount from front and back while serging.

6. Serge at a slow to moderate speed.

7. Gently stretch the edge after serging to increase the lettuce effect.

Note from Nancy

It helps to lower the differential feed, if available, to a minus number (about 0.6mm) when serging a lettuce edge.

Picot edging

The blind hem stitch makes an attractive picot edge on soft and lightweight knits with ample stretch such as tricot, interlock and lightweight spandex knits.

1. Fold a ½" (13mm) hem to the wrong side of the fabric.

2. Place the fabric wrong side up to the right of the needle, so that the left swing of the stitch goes past the edge of the hem to the left of the foot.

3. Finger press the hem in place.

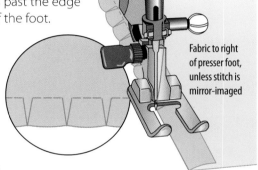

Fabric to right of presser foot, unless stitch is mirror-imaged

4. When stitching, the zigzag of the blind hem stitch should just clear the fabric folded edge, creating the picot edge.

5. For a more defined picot edge, set the blind hem to a 5mm width and a 1.5mm length. For a smaller picot edge, use a zigzag stitch width of 5mm and a length of 2mm.

6. Trim away excess fabric in the hem area, if desired.

Note from Nancy

If you have a mirror image feature on your sewing machine, use it so that you are able to keep the fabric to the left of the needle, as usual. The right swing of the stitch should go slightly past the edge of the fabric.

Note from Nancy

Make sure the tension is balanced when stitching is done on the wrong side of the fabric.

Cutting it close

Trim close to the stitching by "beveling" the scissors or by using appliqué scissors. To bevel the scissors, place them on the same plane as the fabric to allow the blade of the scissors to lie extremely close to the stitching. Cut carefully.

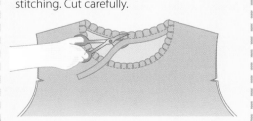

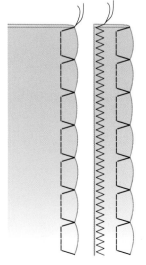

Picot piping

Picot edging can also be applied to piping, and used in place of regular piping in a seam or neck edge for a decorative appearance.

1. Cut bias strips of knit 2"–2½" (5cm to 6cm) wide, and as long as desired.

2. Fold bias strips in half, wrong sides together. Create a picot edge along the fold using a wide width, about 5mm, and a stitch length of about 2mm. You may want to increase the top tension slightly on firmer knit fabrics.

3. Trim the piping to about ½" (13mm) wide, and finish raw edges, if desired.

Ruffles and flounces

Ruffles are fabric strips that are gathered or pleated, whereas flounces are formed by the shape or curve of the fabric piece. Both are attached to another piece of fabric for a fluttery soft edge. Achieve great looking ruffles and flounces with these techniques.

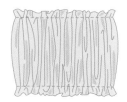

Ruffles

Ruffles can be wide or narrow, ruffled on one or both long edges, and edges may be finished in many different ways. The amount of gathering and edge finishing determines how soft and full the sweep of the ruffle becomes.

1. Determine the ruffling strip sizes.

- On knit fabrics, there is usually no need to cut fabric strips for ruffles on the bias, unless the fabric is overly stiff or heavy.
- The width of the ruffle is determined by the project it is used on; however, a wide ruffle needs to be gathered tighter than a narrow ruffle to achieve what looks like the same amount of fullness.
- To determine the length of strips to cut for gathering, measure the edge of the project where the ruffle will be attached. Multiply 1.5 times that amount to find a measurement for a slightly gathered ruffle, 2 times that measurement for moderate fullness, and 3 times the measurement for generous gathers (see sidebar).
- Cut the number of strips needed to achieve the fullness desired.
- Stitch crossgrain strips together with a straight seam, and bias strips with the strip edges at a 45° angle.

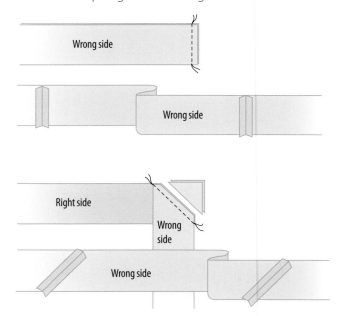

The length of fabric needed for the ruffle

For example, if the edge of the project measures 20" (51cm), then:

For a slightly gathered ruffle:
1.5 x 20" (51cm) = 30" (76.5cm) long strip

For moderate fullness:
2 x 20" (51cm) = 40" (102cm) long strip

For generous gathers:
3 x 20" (51cm) = 60" (153cm) long strip

2. Finish the edges of the ruffling strips using one of the following methods on knits.

Raw edges: Knits don't ravel, and it's totally acceptable to leave the edges raw. A raw-edged ruffle tends to look fuller because it is lighter in weight than a finished edge.

Pinked edges: A pinked edge produces a sawtooth look that may add to the design of various projects. Pinked edges may also be clipped between the points of the edging to create a fringe-like appearance.

Fused edges: Apply a narrow paper-backed fusible web to the wrong side of the ruffle hem. Then remove paper, turn narrow hem toward the wrong side of the ruffle, and press. See page 66 for this fusible hemming technique.

Binding: Use a bias-cut binding (page 87) or a knit binding (page 78) to finish the edges of the ruffle. See page 53 for more information on bindings for knits.

Serged edge: Use a narrow 3-thread overlock, a rolled edge or a lettuce edge (page 80), as desired.

3. Gather the ruffling strips to equal the measurement of the edge to which it will be attached. There are three main methods for gathering fabric.

Hand gathering: Use a heavy thread, and start with a knot in the end of the thread to secure the ending point of the stitching. Hand stitch a single row of running stitches ⅛"–¼" (3mm to 6mm) from the edge of the fabric. Pull up the stitches to draw the fabric up into a gathered edge.

Machine gathering: Zigzag over a heavy cording that is at least 12" (31cm) longer than the measurement of the area to which the ruffle will be attached. Use straight pins to hold the excess cording on each end of the ruffle by twisting the cording around the pin several times in a figure-eight movement.

Gathering with specialty feet such as a gathering foot or a ruffler attachment: See information included with these feet for use with your machine.

Pinked edge

Pinked edge clipped for fringe

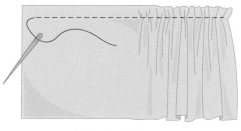

Hand-gathered edge

Zigzag over cord

Machine-gathered edge

Note from Nancy

Fabric may also be gathered using various elastic techniques (see page 39).

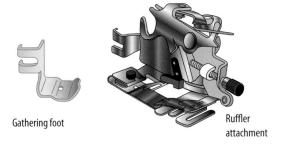

Gathering foot

Ruffler attachment

4. Attach ruffling strip.

- Pin the gathered edge of the ruffling strip to the project, right sides together.
- Distribute gathers evenly.
- Baste into position.
- Stitch.
- Press seam allowance toward the project.

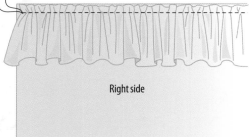

Right side

Note from Nancy

To attach multiple ruffling strips for a tiered look, place the ruffles on the right side of the project and stitch into position with a straight stitch. Each ruffle overlaps the ruffle below it, covering the raw edge of the previous ruffle. The top edge may be finished with trim or hidden in a band or seam.

Note from Nancy

Add a ruffle to your favorite knit top for a quick feminine touch. Gather a 2½" (6cm) strip of crinkled chiffon, about ½" (13mm) from the top edge, and pink the raw edges for a softer look. Stitch the ruffle to the front neckline over the gathering thread.

Flounces

A flounce, or flowing trim, can be wide, narrow or shaped. Plus, the edges may be finished in many different ways.

1. Create flounce patterns.

Curved (the most subtle flounce): Determine the length of the flounce, and draw a rectangle that length by the desired width. Slash the rectangle every 1"–2" (3cm to 5cm), and spread the pattern piece. Round out the curve.

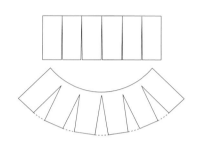

Circular (the easiest flounce):

- Use a yardstick compass or circle ruler to draw a large circle on paper.
- Draw a smaller circle inside the large circle. The circumference of the inner circle is the length of the flounce. Mark an opening.
- Create a length of trim similar to a ruffle when the open center circular flounce is clipped. The smaller the inner circle radius, the fuller the flounce.
- Cut half circles if you don't have enough fabric to cut circle flounces, as long as the grainline (crosswise or lengthwise) is balanced, or in the same direction on the multiple flounce sections. Add seam allowances. Stitch the circular flounce sections together, as shown. Spread seamed flounce sections to cover the project. Baste in place.

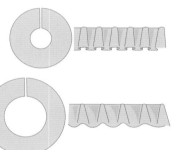

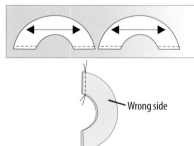

Balance grainlines

Wrong side

Spiral circle (the most dramatic flounce with a gradated width):

- Draw a circle and mark the center.
- Start cutting a flounce on the outside edge of the circle, trimming in a circular fashion in a counterclockwise direction.
- Cut flounce about 2½" (6cm) wide at the widest part of the strip, and taper to about ¾" (19mm) at each end. Or, make your own variation.

Note from Nancy

An outer circle with a diameter of 20½" (52cm) and an inner circle with a diameter of 13½" (34cm) will yield a 3" (8cm) wide flounce that is long enough to attach to a 44" (112cm) length of fabric.

Squares, triangles, swirls and other shapes: Attach shapes to a neckline, down a seam or in another area of a garment so that they are allowed to drape. Shaped flounces may be tacked in one place or attached with a single row of stitching.

2. Finish the edges of knit flounces using one of the following methods.

Raw edge: Many of the new knit fashions leave the edges raw. A raw-edged flounce tends to drape better because it is lighter in weight than an edge that has a finish.

Pinked edge: A pinked edge produces a sawtooth look that may add some pizzazz to various projects.

Serged edge: Use a narrow 3-thread overlock, a rolled edge or a lettuce edge (page 80), as desired.

3. Attach raw flounce edges.

- Use a regular stitch length, as a short stitch tends to stiffen the flounce seam.
- Pin raw edges of flounce to the garment, right sides together, and stitch. Press seam toward garment.
- Flip the flounce over the seam. Topstitch close to the seam, catching the seam allowance.

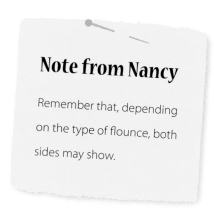

Note from Nancy

Remember that, depending on the type of flounce, both sides may show.

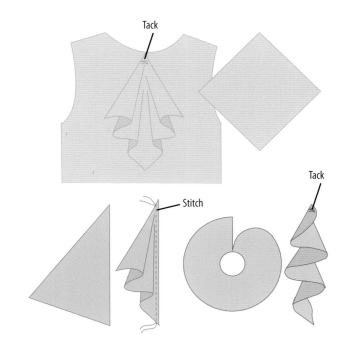

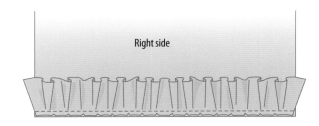

Pin raw edges of flounce to garment, right sides together; stitch

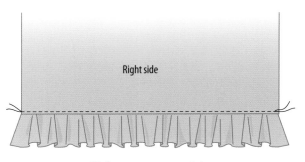

Flip flounce over seam; topstitch

Lightweight crosswise binding strips

Trim the free edges of knits with a lightweight knit fabric. Choose inconspicuous colors, or "go for the bold" and choose knit fabrics that make a statement. Either way, this technique makes knit trim/binding easy to stitch.

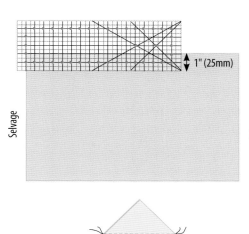

1. Cut 1" (25mm) crosswise strips of lightweight knit with at least 25% stretch. Use the straight bottom edge of a quilting ruler to cut crosswise knit strips.

2. Join ends of the strips diagonally, right sides together, to make ample trim to finish the edges of your project.

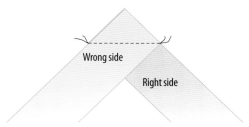

3. Attach trim.

- Stitch trim to fabric, right sides together, with a ¼" (6mm) seam.

- Press trim to the wrong side of the project, with approximately ¼" (6mm) of trim showing on the right side; pin in place.

- Stitch in the ditch of the seam. Remove pins.

- Trim excess binding close to the stitching on the wrong side, if desired, with appliqué scissors. The beveled edge prevents you from cutting into your project as you trim the seam close to the stitching.

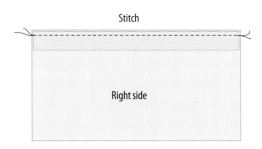

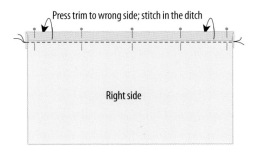

Note from Nancy

Add a touch of color by choosing bias trim cut from woven fabric. Cut the 1" (25mm) strips on the bias as shown.

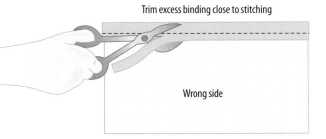

Hand stitches

Blanket stitch

This is a preferred edge for lightweight fleece blankets and garments. Use yarn or heavy thread for blanket stitches. You have no worries about trying to pull yarn or thread through the fabric if you use the specialty Edge Perfect Blade to precut fabric.

1. Precut fabric.

- Place the Edge Perfect Blade on any 45mm rotary cutter.
- Align a straightedge ruler ½" (13mm) from the edge of the fabric.
- Cut along the edge of the ruler with the Edge Perfect Blade. It makes perfectly spaced holes ⅜" (10mm) apart, eliminating the need to prepunch holes with an awl or punch.

2. Thread a hand sewing needle with several strands of floss, decorative thread or yarn.

3. Stitch.

- Anchor the first stitch at the edge of the fabric, starting in an inconspicuous area.
- Work from left to right, inserting the needle into the precut holes. It's important that the point of the needle goes over the thread loop that forms.
- Repeat, placing a blanket stitch at each precut hole.
- After the last stitch, tie off the thread in an inconspicuous area and cut the thread.

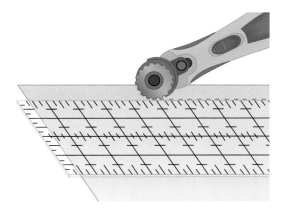

Whipstitch

A whipstitch is more of a wrapped stitch than a blanket stitch, and it doesn't have a thread along the edge of the project.

1. Precut fabric following instructions for the blanket stitch.

2. Thread a hand sewing needle with several strands of floss, decorative thread or yarn.

3. Use the same stitching process as for the blanket stitch, except that the point of the needle does not go over the thread loop as you stitch.

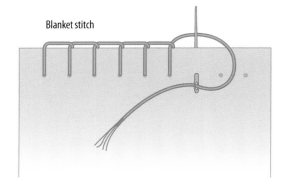

Blanket stitch

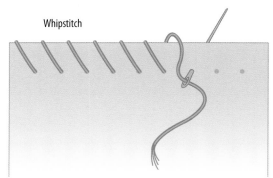

Whipstitch

3-D flower embellishments

"Flower power" is back, and this time there's a plethora of blooming options! We've included some fast and feminine versions for a flower fantasia suitable for artful clothing and accessories.

Tee rosettes

Use leftover knit fabric to make whisper-soft tee rosettes, perfect for embellishing a T-shirt or accessory.

1. Cut bias strips.

- Cut one bias strip each of the following widths: ¾" (19mm), 1" (25mm) and 1½" (38mm) long for three differently sized rosettes, as shown.

- Subcut the strips in 7"–8" (18cm to 20cm) lengths for each rosette.

- Trim one edge of each strip with a pinking or scalloping rotary blade.

2. Add Fuse 'n Gather tape to each bias strip for gathering the rosettes.

- Cut a 9" (23cm) strip of tape for each rosette.

- Press the tape to the wrong side of each bias strip with blue threads right side up, aligning one long edge to the edge of the fabric strip. Extend the tape ½" (13mm) beyond each bias strip on the short edges.

- Pull the blue threads out of the tape ¼" (6mm) from each end of the bias strip.

Note from Nancy

Clover's Fuse 'n Gather is an ideal timesaver when creating this embellishment. Simply fuse tape into position and pull the blue threads to gather.

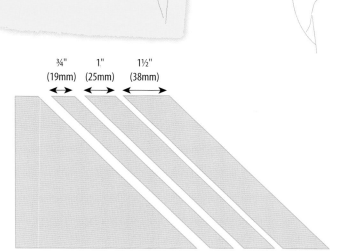

¾" (19mm) 1" (25mm) 1½" (38mm)

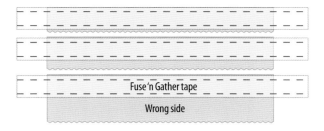

Fuse 'n Gather tape

Wrong side

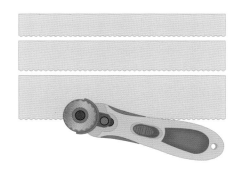

Pull out threads ¼" (6mm) on each end

- Carefully trim the excess tape from each edge, being careful not to trim the threads.

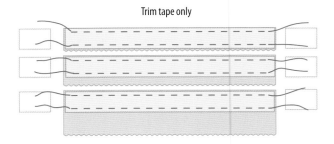

Trim tape only

3. Complete the rosette.

- Stitch the strip into a circle, meeting short ends and taking a ¼" (6mm) seam. Be careful not to catch the blue thread ends of the Fuse 'n Gather in the seam.

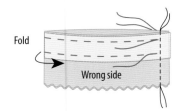

Fold

Wrong side

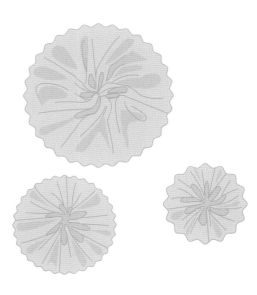

- Secure the threads around a pin at one edge of the tape. Pull the free ends of the blue threads on the opposite edge to gather the fabric.

- Using the threads from the gathering tape, hand stitch the embellishment into a rosette. If gathering threads aren't long enough, use matching thread and a hand stitching needle.

- Hand stitch the tee rosettes to the neckline of a knit top, as shown, or embellish a headband, purse or other project with these dainty blooms.

Blooming buds

Use scraps of lustrous organza or lightweight knit for buds that form a floral necklace on your favorite T-shirt.

1. Create blooming bud flowers.

- Cut a 2¼" (6cm) circle for each blooming bud.
- Fold buds in half, and then in half again.

2. Make a blooming bud flower
arrangement at the neckline of your favorite knit top.

- Arrange 3 or 4 buds to form a flower, with the points of the buds toward the center.
- Bartack the point of each bud to the top.

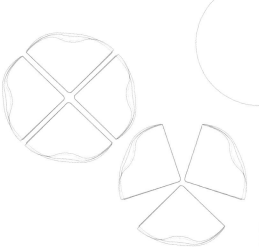

Fold

Fold

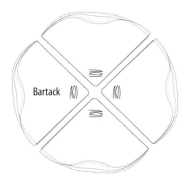

Bartack

Note from Nancy

Add a blooming bud flower and a couple of single buds on the back neckline of the top. Then you'll look good coming and going.

Pleated posies

Cotton batik or lightweight knit creates these tumbling petals. A stiletto or a bamboo cocktail skewer guides the pleats as you stitch for a beautiful texture.

1. Create the pleated posie pattern.

- Cut a 2" × 2¾" (5cm × 7cm) rectangle for each pleated posie.
- Fold the rectangle vertically, then horizontally.
- Measure up ⅝" (16mm) from the left edge; mark.

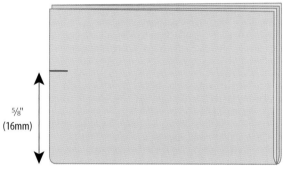

- Trim petal as shown from the bottom fold (right side) around the top, and meeting the ⅝" (16mm) mark on the left side. As in nature, no two blooms are alike.
- Repeat, forming a multitude of posies (19 were used in the T-shirt design on the opposite page).

2. Cut several matching or contrasting leaves, using the pattern shown.

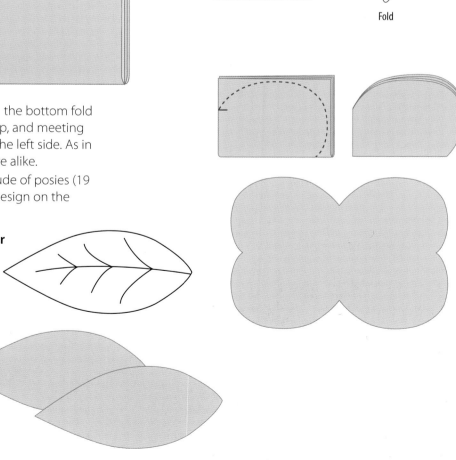

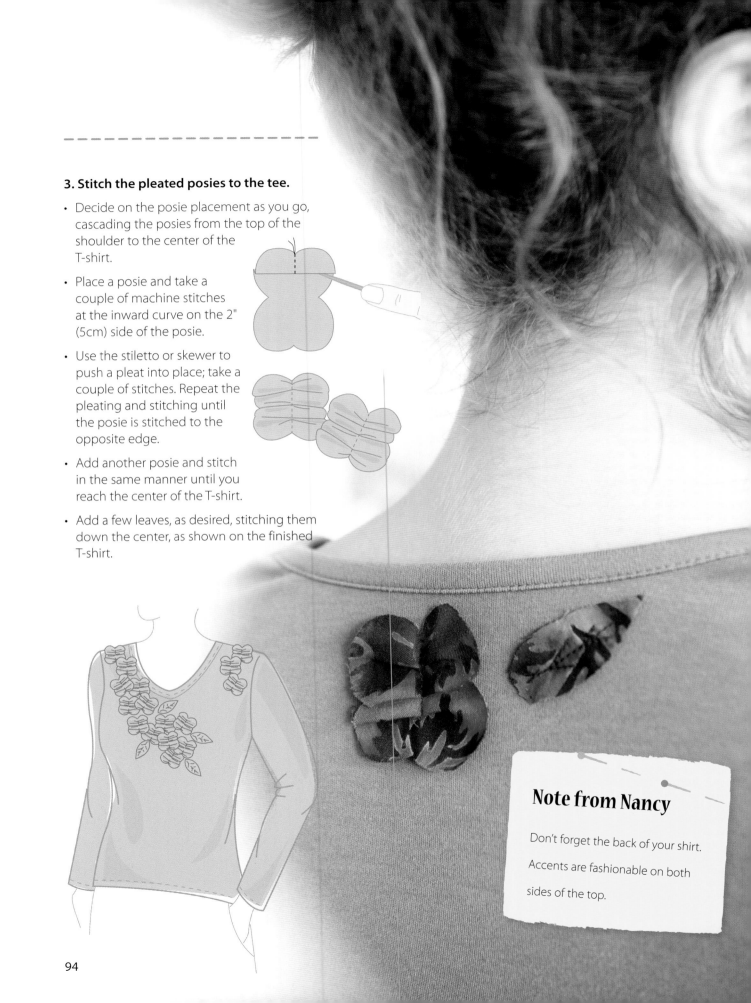

3. Stitch the pleated posies to the tee.

- Decide on the posie placement as you go, cascading the posies from the top of the shoulder to the center of the T-shirt.

- Place a posie and take a couple of machine stitches at the inward curve on the 2" (5cm) side of the posie.

- Use the stiletto or skewer to push a pleat into place; take a couple of stitches. Repeat the pleating and stitching until the posie is stitched to the opposite edge.

- Add another posie and stitch in the same manner until you reach the center of the T-shirt.

- Add a few leaves, as desired, stitching them down the center, as shown on the finished T-shirt.

Note from Nancy

Don't forget the back of your shirt. Accents are fashionable on both sides of the top.

Embroidery on knits

Less is best when it comes to stitching knits, whether selecting a pattern, seaming garment sections or adding embellishment. Embroidery adds an attractive accent to knit garments, but selecting an appropriate design makes all the difference in the finished appearance.

1. Add the embroidery before stitching the seams.

2. Hoop the stabilizer.

- Instead of directly hooping the fabric, hoop a water-activated stabilizer such as hydro-stick. Sometimes two layers of the stabilizer are required to provide adequate support.
- Lightly moisten the hydro-stick stabilizer, using a sponge. The stabilizer becomes sticky.
- Adhere the fabric to be embroidered over the sticky stabilizer, right side up.

3. Embroider the design.

- Set up the machine for embroidery according to instructions in the owner's manual. Use a titanium needle. Titanium extends needle life. These strong, durable needles provide smooth stitching with no thread fraying. Use a lightweight bobbin thread.
- Position the template for the design on the fabric; tape or pin it in place.
- Import the design, position the needle at the center point, and remove the template.
- Add a water-soluble stabilizer on top of the fabric for added stability.
- Stitch design(s).
- Remove the top stabilizer. Remove the interior of the stabilizer by spritzing it with water.
- Remove the stabilizer from the hoop.
- Gently lift and trim the optional no-show fusible mesh stabilizer.
- Rinse away any excess water-soluble stabilizer used as a topping for the embroidery.

Note from Nancy

I prefer to add a layer of no-show fusible mesh stabilizer directly to the wrong side of the T-shirt in the embroidery area for extra support. This stabilizer also protects the T-shirt from undo stress when removing the hydro-stick stabilizer, and it can be gently peeled back and trimmed after the embroidery is complete.

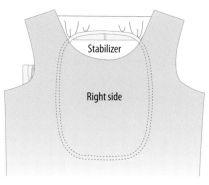

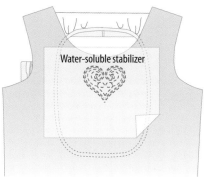

Note from Nancy

Avoid dense embroidery that might distort and overpower the knit fabric. Choose a light embroidery instead. Selecting only the outline of a traditional embroidery or portions of the design works best.

Embroidering on a ready-made T-shirt

1. Find and mark the center of the T-shirt front.

2. Press a no-show fusible mesh stabilizer to the wrong side of the T-shirt in the embroidery area.

Mesh stabilizer

Wrong side

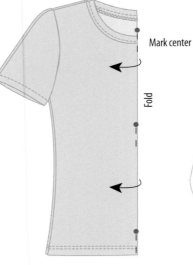

Mark center

Fold

3. Place a target sticker (for crosshair marking) on the right side in the center of the embroidery area using an embroidery template for positioning, if desired.

4. Prepare for embroidery.

- Hoop hydro-stick stabilizer.
- Place hooped stabilizer at the end of an ironing board.
- Bring T-shirt over the end of the ironing board and the hoop. Match the target sticker on the T-shirt and the center of the hoop.
- Moisten and adhere fabric as shown on page 95.
- Bring the back and sides of the T-shirt up and over the ironing board, around hoop.

Target sticker

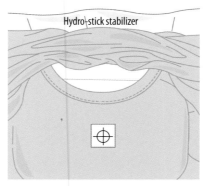

Hydro-stick stabilizer

Bring back and sides of T-shirt around hoop

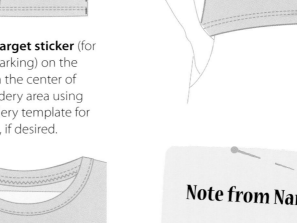

Note from Nancy

More is better when it comes to stabilizer. The embroidery is simple; getting the fabrics stable is what sometimes takes a bit of knowledge.

5. Embroider the design, being careful not to catch the back or sides of the T-shirt in the embroidery.

6. Remove the embroidery from the hoop, and remove the excess stabilizer.

- Tear away the excess hydro-stick stabilizer.
- Gently release and trim the excess no-show fusible mesh stabilizer.

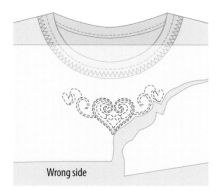

Wrong side

Chapter 5

Knit Projects

Use your newfound knowledge to sew quick and easy projects. We've included a pair of texting gloves, a cowl scarf, a flouncy tee, a T-shirt makeover and a no-slip wrap. These simple projects are fun to make for yourself or as gifts. Jump on the bandwagon of fashion and sew knits with confidence.

Fleece texting gloves

Small pieces of fleece fabric are ideal for the quickest of all fleece accessories—texting gloves. There are really only three steps: cut, stitch and turn.

Supplies

- ✓ ½ yard (.5m) high-loft fleece
- ✓ Matching all-purpose thread
- ✓ Pattern paper and marker
- ✓ Double-stick fusible web sheets

Fleece texting gloves

Prepare the pattern

1. Trace a 12" × 14" (31cm × 36cm) rectangle, with the grain running the 14" (36cm) length.

2. Measure in 1" (25mm) from each edge at one 12" (31cm) end. Draw a line from the point to the other 12" (31cm) end, tapering the pattern.

3. Mark a 1" (25mm) seam allowance along the 14" (36cm) edges. Also mark a thumb opening 2" (5cm) and 4½" (11cm) from the narrower end of the glove.

Cut out two fleece sections using the pattern

1. Clip to seam allowance at marked thumb openings. Use double-stick fusible web sheets to turn under the seam allowance.

2. Stitch the seam allowance in place.

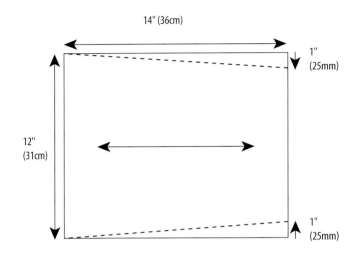

14" (36cm)

1" (25mm)

12" (31cm)

1" (25mm)

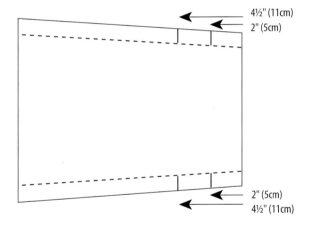

4½" (11cm)
2" (5cm)

2" (5cm)
4½" (11cm)

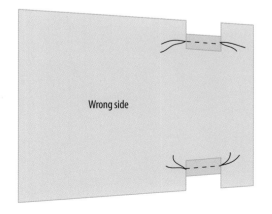

Wrong side

Stitch the gloves

1. Meet the long edges, right sides together. Stitch 1" (25mm) seam with a basting stitch. Remember not to sew in the thumb area.

Note from Nancy

Before doing the final hemming, try on the gloves and check the fit. Adjust the seam allowance, taking a narrower or deeper seam if needed.

2. Restitch the seam, reinforcing stitching before and after the thumb opening.

3. Turn under a ⅝" (16mm) hem at the upper and lower edges of the gloves. Topstitch.

4. Turn the gloves right side out.

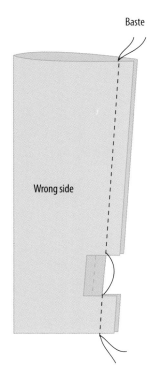

Baste

Wrong side

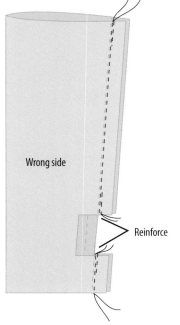

Wrong side

Reinforce

Wrong side

Turn ends under and topstitch

Cowl scarf

Cozy without being bulky—that's what best describes this cowl scarf. Snapped closed under a coat or jacket, this scarf hugs your neckline without layers. If buttons are more your style, add detail with easy-to-sew buttonholes designed specifically for knits.

Supplies

- ✓ ½ yard (.5m) high-loft fleece
- ✓ Matching all-purpose thread
- ✓ Matching woolly nylon thread (optional)
- ✓ Snaps or buttons
- ✓ Rotary cutter (with decorative scallop blade)
- ✓ Ruler
- ✓ Cutting mat

Cowl scarf

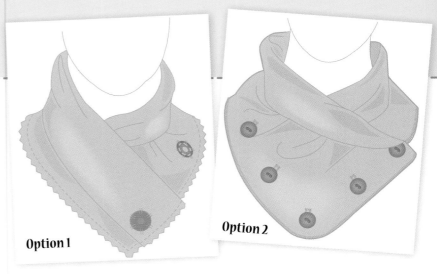

Option 1

Option 2

Instructions

1. Cut an 18" × 36" (46cm × 91cm) rectangle, with the more stable grain in the 18" (46cm) direction.

2. Construct the cowl using one of the following options.

Option 1

1. Fold the rectangle in half, wrong sides together, meeting 36" (91cm) edges.

2. Straight stitch ½" (13mm) from the cut edges.

3. Add a decorative finish by trimming edges with a decorative rotary blade.

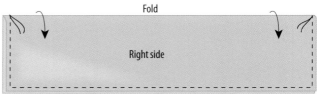

Fold

Right side

Decorative edge

Note from Nancy

For best results when cutting multiple layers of fleece with a rotary cutter, position the blade at a 90° angle to the cutting surface and press down firmly as you cut.

4. Overlap short ends, aligning the 9" (23cm) edge at one end with the 36" (91cm) edge at the other end, to create an "L" shape.

5. Hand stitch three large snaps at the overlap, positioning two of them along the 9" (23cm) edge and the third about 8" (20cm) from the short edge. Reposition the ends of the scarf and stitch the second half of each snap at the corresponding position on the second end of the scarf.

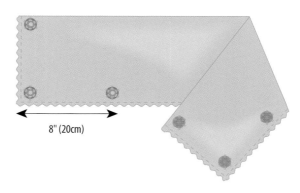

8" (20cm)

Option 2

1. If the fabric has a tendency to ravel, finish the edges.

2. Fold the rectangle in half, wrong sides together, meeting 36" (91cm) edges.

3. Shape lower corners using a Round The Corner ruler or a dessert plate.

4. Straight stitch edges together close to the cut edges.

5. Adjust the serger for a 3-thread overlock stitch, threading the loopers with woolly nylon and the needle with all-purpose thread. The texturized woolly nylon thread fills in the stitching, and provides lots of give and stretch.

6. Test stitching on a fabric sample; serge outer edges.

7. Add a drop of liquid seam sealant such as Fray Check or Fray Block to thread tails. After the seam sealant has dried, clip off the excess threads or bury them in the stitching.

8. Add three to five buttonholes. Position one buttonhole at the curved corner and one or two on each side in the cowl overlap area. (Those shown are positioned about 3½" [9cm] apart on the 9" [23cm] edge and the adjoining edge, but feel free to position the buttonholes as desired.)

- Select a stretch buttonhole. Stitches are less dense and farther apart than for a buttonhole intended for a woven fabric.
- Place a water-soluble stabilizer on top of and underneath the fabric as you stitch.
- Stitch and open the buttonholes (see page 62).

9. Overlap the cowl and stitch buttons in position, corresponding to the buttonholes.

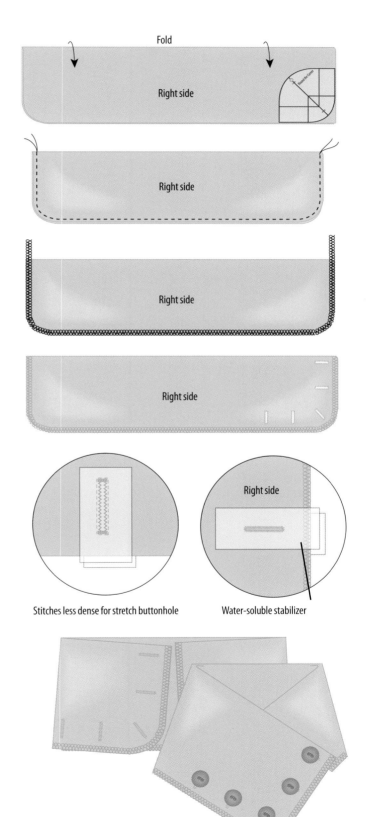

Stitches less dense for stretch buttonhole

Water-soluble stabilizer

T-shirt makeover

Are you looking to make your favorite T-shirt pattern, but can't find the right fabric? Check out ready-to-wear clothing for a knit top in just the right color and fabric. Two purchased knit tops often offer the same options as a yard of fabric. There are bonuses to this type of "yardage"—you are able to use the finished neckline and hemline of the ready-to-wear tops. That means less actual sewing time! Plus, you can adjust the pattern in just the right places for a perfect fit or change the length of the sleeves or hem. You'll have yardage left for simple accents, such as fabric flowers added to the neckline.

Supplies

- ✓ Two knit tops: Purchase one top in your size (Top A) and the other (Top B) in the largest size available to provide more yardage
- ✓ Your favorite T-shirt pattern, in just the right size
- ✓ Matching all-purpose thread
- ✓ Fuse 'n Gather tape
- ✓ Water-erasable fabric marker

T-shirt makeover

Instructions

Note: All seams are ¼" (6mm) unless otherwise stated.

1. Cut Top A apart along each side and underarm seam.

2. Use T-shirt pattern front to create a new front for Top A.

- Fold Top A in half, meeting side edges, shoulder seams and center front.
- Overlay T-shirt pattern on Top A, matching center fronts and shoulder seams.
- Pin pattern to fabric.

3. Trim Top A (front) to match pattern along side seams and armholes.

Cut along each side and underarm seam

Top A

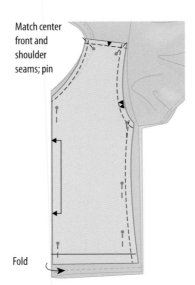

Match center front and shoulder seams; pin

Fold

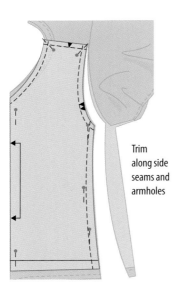

Trim along side seams and armholes

4. Measure the difference between the length of the finished top and the pattern. In some instances, the top may be shorter than the pattern. In this example, the top is longer than the pattern.

Note from Nancy

Mark pattern notches on the new Top A using a water-erasable fabric marker. These marks help with matching as you sew the armhole and side seams.

Note from Nancy

A 1" (25mm) difference in length is not going to make a significant change to the top. For a timesaving step, utilize the hem of the finished top.

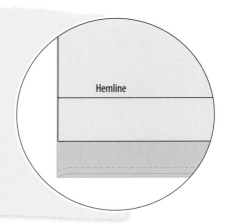

Hemline

5. Use the T-shirt pattern back to create a new back for Top A.

- Refold Top A, aligning side edges, shoulder seam and center back.
- Overlay T-shirt back pattern, matching center back and shoulder seam allowances with Top A. Pin pattern to Top A.

6. Trim Top A (back) to match pattern along side seams and armholes. Mark notches.

7. Create new sleeves using Top B as fabric yardage.

- Place Top B on cutting surface, aligning hem edges.
- Place the hemline of T-shirt sleeve pattern along finished hem of Top B.
- Cut out the sleeve pattern shapes. Mark notches.
- Save the remaining fabric from Top B for embellishment.

8. Optional: Add floral embellishments such as tee rosettes. Use Fuse 'n Gather tape to gather the rosettes quickly, as shown on page 89.

9. Set sleeves into armholes.

- Align sleeve to armhole, matching right sides and notches. See information for knit seams on page 36.
- Stitch or serge the sleeve armhole on the new sleeves to Top A.
- Prepare and stitch underarm seams.

(1) Align edges at both the sleeve and lower hemlines. Pin. Since the hemlines are already finished, take extra time to align the edges of the finished hemlines.

(2) Stitch or serge underarm seams, removing pins as you stitch.

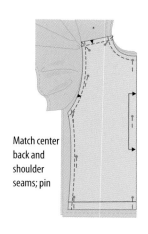

Match center back and shoulder seams; pin

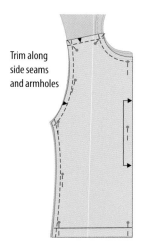

Trim along side seams and armholes

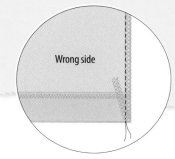

Note from Nancy

If seams are serged, stitch the serger thread into the seam with a straight stitch. Clip off excess thread tails.

Stitch serger thread into seam

Wrong side

Wrong side

Align edges of finished hemlines

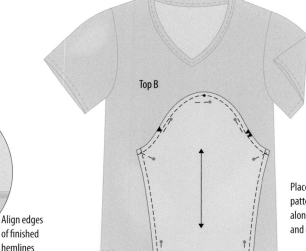

Top B

Place sleeve pattern hemline along finished hem and cut sleeves

Flouncy tee

The feather-light flounces created for this tee are raw-edged and easy to achieve. Use your favorite knit top pattern and these instructions to conjure up a top with charming details—skinny rows of flounces.

Supplies

✓ T-shirt pattern

✓ Matching all-purpose thread

✓ 2 yards (1.8m) lightweight knit fabric

✓ Pattern paper

✓ 24" (61cm) clear ruler

Flouncy tee

Prepare the pattern

1. Trace the T-shirt front on pattern paper; trim off excess paper.

2. Transfer markings.

3. Fold the side seams to the center front at the hemline, and crease the paper. Fold a second time, and place a mark at the first and second creases on each side of the center front.

T-shirt front

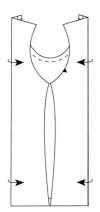 

Fold side seams to center front

Fold again

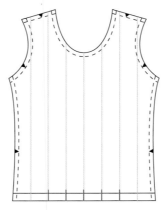

Unfold and mark first and second creases from center

4. Measure 1" (25mm) and 2" (5cm) from the center front along the neckline.

5. Align ruler between the first marking along the neckline and the first marking at the hemline. Draw a line between the two marks. Repeat for the second set of markings.

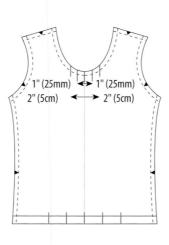

1" (25mm) 1" (25mm)
2" (5cm)   2" (5cm)

6. Draw grainlines parallel to the center front in the middle and side pieces. Mark pattern pieces.

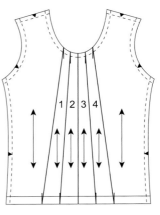

1 2 3 4

7. Cut out the pattern.

8. Add ¼" (6mm) seam allowances along all vertical seams with the exception of the side seams, which already have seam allowances.

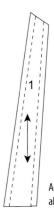

Add seam allowances

Create flounces

1. Cut five 8½" (22cm) circles.

2. Start cutting a flounce on the outside edge of a circle, trimming in a circular fashion in a counterclockwise direction. Cut the flounce about 2½" (6cm) wide at the widest part of the strip, and taper to ¾" (19mm) at the inside of the circle. Repeat for the remaining circles.

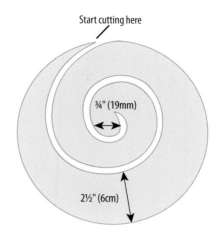

Start cutting here

¾" (19mm)

2½" (6cm)

Complete the flouncy top

1. Slip a flounce between each of the center seams, positioning the wider end of the flounce 1" (25mm) above the 1" (25mm) hemline and the top of the flounce ½" to ¾" (13mm to 19mm) from the neckline, depending on what is allowed for finishing the neckline on the pattern. Pin in place.

2. Stitch seams.

3. Complete the garment following pattern instructions.

4. Press and topstitch a 1" (25mm) hem into position. Trim excess fabric from the hem.

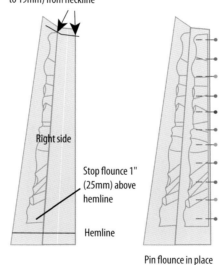

Start flounce ½" to ¾" (13mm to 19mm) from neckline

Right side

Stop flounce 1" (25mm) above hemline

Hemline

Pin flounce in place

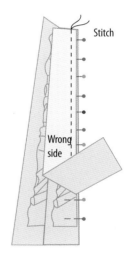

Stitch

Wrong side

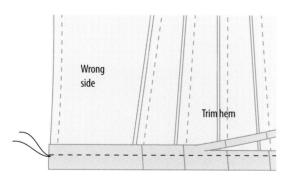

Wrong side

Trim hem

Note from Nancy

Take care when stitching the neckline and hem so that the edges of the flounces aren't caught in the stitching.

No-slip wrap

When you feel chilled, the best way to be comfy is to layer with a fleece wrap. Designed to hug your shoulders, this wrap will assuredly stay in place. See how easily you can make this no-slip wrap.

Supplies

- ✓ 1½ yards (1.4m) fleecy fabric
- ✓ Matching all-purpose thread
- ✓ Large button
- ✓ Rotary cutter
- ✓ Cutting mat
- ✓ Ruler

No-slip wrap

Cut, stitch and shape the fabric

1. Cut one rectangle 20" × 54" (51cm × 137cm), and a second rectangle 20" × 34" (51cm × 86cm). Cut with the more stable grain going the length of the rectangle.

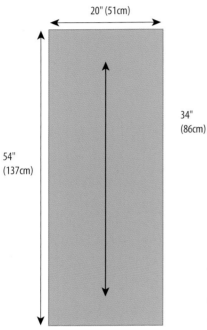

20" (51cm)

54" (137cm)

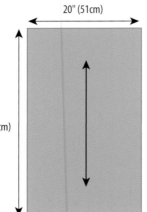

20" (51cm)

34" (86cm)

2. Position the two rectangles on top of one another, right sides together, meeting the 20" (51cm) edge of the smaller rectangle to a 54" (137cm) edge of the larger rectangle to create an "L" shape.

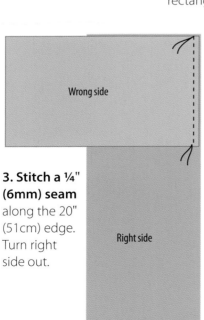

Wrong side

Right side

3. Stitch a ¼" (6mm) seam along the 20" (51cm) edge. Turn right side out.

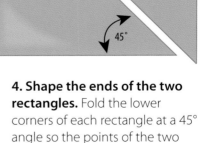

Right side

45°

45°

4. Shape the ends of the two rectangles. Fold the lower corners of each rectangle at a 45° angle so the points of the two rectangles are at the center front, and trim away excess fabric.

Finish the edges of the wrap

1. Adjust the sewing machine for a straight stitch with a stitch length of approximately 3mm.

2. Insert a stretch needle. A stretch needle has a ballpoint tip that gently spreads the fleece fibers apart, rather than piercing them. The long flat shank allows the needle to pass close to the bobbin and decreases skipped stitches.

3. Turn under ¼" to ⅜" (6mm to 10mm) on the wrap's outer edges and topstitch.

Note from Nancy

If the edges of the fleece ravel, you may want to serge the edge before hemming.

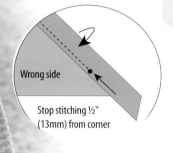

Wrong side

Stop stitching ½" (13mm) from corner

4. At the 45° angle corners, turn under and stitch the hem on one edge. Stop stitching ½" (13mm) from the corner.

Trim excess

5. Fold under the second edge of the 45° angle and trim excess hem allowance.

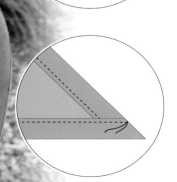

6. Continue stitching the remainder of the hem.

7. Repeat on the second 45° angle.

Add an optional closure

1. Try on the wrap. Position a large button at a convenient location for the closing. (There is no specific location for the button. It's your personal choice.)

2. Hand stitch the button to the wrap, adding a small rectangle of fabric behind the button for added support.

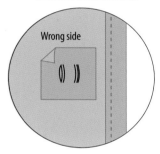

Wrong side

3. Make a button loop:

- Cut a fabric tube approximately 1½" × 6" (38mm × 15cm). (Size the loop to fit the button.)
- Meet outer 6" (15cm) edges to the center of the strip.
- Fold the strip in half, meeting folded edges.
- Stitch along the folded edges.

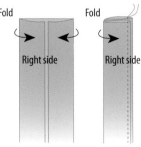

Fold | Fold

Right side | Right side

4. Tack the loop to the right front of the wrap, positioning and sizing it to accommodate the button. Edgestitch loop in place.

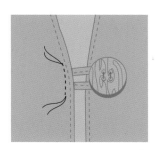

Glossary

Acrylic: A synthetic or man-made fiber that mimics the characteristics of many different fibers. Acrylic is commonly used in knit fabrics that are lightweight, soft and warm. Some fabrications may pill easily. Acrylic fibers take color well, are washable and are generally hypoallergenic.

Appliqué scissors: Specialty scissors designed for trimming close to stitching; especially useful to trim knit hems. One blade of this scissors has a "bill" that lifts the section being trimmed without nicking the fabric underneath.

Baby elastic: Soft, stretchy elastic (55% polyester/45% rubber) typically ⅛" (3mm) wide; used for necklines, sleeves and other areas where you would use a small casing. Or, zigzag the elastic directly to the wrong side of the project.

Ballpoint needle: Needle with a rounded tip to prevent snags and holes on knit fabrics. A ballpoint needle is especially good to use on sweater knits, as it separates the knit fibers rather than piercing them.

Baste: Using long hand or sewing machine stitches to temporarily hold two or more layers of fabric together.

Berber knit: A sherpa-like fleece composed of blended fibers. Berber may be a polyester blend or acrylic. Right and wrong sides are usually different; sometimes berber has a knit backing.

Bias: True bias forms a 45° angle to the lengthwise and crosswise threads in a fabric. Bias-cut woven binding may be used to finish the edges on a variety of knit fabrics.

Binding: Fabric strips that are sewn to the edge of a project to finish the edge or add a decorative accent.

Blanket stitch: A hand stitch using heavy thread or yarn to overcast the edge of blankets and clothing, especially preferred for lightweight fleece.

Blind hem foot: Foot that positions and holds fabric straight when hemming. The blind hem stitch includes several straight stitches followed by one zigzag stitch, repeated along the entire hem. This stitch is almost invisible on the right side of the fabric.

Bodkin: Tool used to grip elastic or trim and feed it through a casing.

Buttonhole elastic: A knitted elastic with buttonholes spaced ½"–1" (13mm to 25mm) apart. This adjustable elastic is perfect for maternity and children's clothes.

Casing: A channel formed by two layers of fabric connected by two or more rows of stitching, in which elastic or a drawstring is inserted.

Clear elastic: 100% polyurethane elastic ¼" or ⅜" (6mm or 10mm) wide that stretches up to three times its original length and retracts to original size when released. Clear elastic is ideal for swimwear, children's garments and stabilizing shoulder seams.

Color-catching laundry sheets: Specially formulated sheets that trap loose dyes in the washer to prevent running or bleeding onto the remaining washload. These sheets are especially good to use when washing a light-colored knit with dark ribbing or trim.

Cover-stitched hem: Resembles the hem produced with a double (or twin) needle, except that it is made on a cover stitch serger. A stitch similar to an overlock is on the reverse side, which incorporates stretch.

Cowl neckline: A large, loosely draped neckline.

Cut-away stabilizer: A type of stabilizer removed by cutting with scissors after embroidery is completed. A cut-away stabilizer is appropriate for delicate fabrics such as knits for designs that might be distorted by tearing away the stabilizer.

Cutting mat: A mat made of special "self-healing" material that is not damaged by the blade of a rotary cutter; often marked with horizontal and vertical lines for ease in measuring. The cutting mat protects the work surface and is a must when using a rotary cutter.

Density: How close together stitches are in an embroidery design; influenced by the number and type of stitches in a design. Less-dense embroidery designs are best for knits.

Double knit: Medium to heavyweight fabric with less than 25% stretch. Double knit has a crosswise stretch, but the length is stable. It looks the same on both front and back, like interlock, but it is much beefier. Use for designs with more body such as jackets, pants, dresses and skirts.

Double needles: Two needles attached to a single shaft (also called twin needles). Double needles make two perfectly parallel rows of stitching on the right side of the fabric. On the wrong side of the fabric, the single bobbin thread produces a zigzag-type stitch, building stretch into the seam or hem.

Drawcord elastic: 66% polyester/34% rubber knit elastic with a polyester drawcord. Comfortable, adjustable and perfect for shorts, pants and other sportswear.

Elastic thread: 28% polyester/72% rubber thread used for gathering, shirring and smocking.

Fantastic Elastic: A 1½" (38mm) wide knit elastic that can be cut down to ¼" (6mm) wide without raveling or compromising the stretch.

Flat construction: Edges are trimmed with binding or ribbing and sleeves are inserted before seams are sewn. Flat construction works exceptionally well for serged knits, doll clothes and children's clothing.

Flounces: Trim formed by the shape or curve of a fabric piece. Attach flounce to another piece of fabric for a soft, fluttery edge.

Fold-over elastic plush: Super-soft elastic with a plush finish on one side (62% nylon/28% polyester/10% spandex). Fold-over elastic creates a soft, flexible finish on knits such as baby clothes and fleece.

French terry: A knit that is smooth on one side with an uncut loop pile on the opposite side. It is usually a little lighter weight than fleece.

Fuse 'n Gather tape: A ⅝" (16mm) wide tape that eliminates the need to sew gathering stitches. Simply press it into position on the wrong side of the fabric, with the blue threads facing up. Pull the blue threads to gather, and stitch to secure gathers or attach to another fabric.

Fuse-pressed hem: A hem that is pressed into position using fusible web instead of or in addition to stitching the fabric.

Fusible knit interfacing: An additional layer of lightweight fusible knit fabric pressed to the wrong side of knit fabrics to add body and stability.

Fusible web: A thin layer of man-made fibers that will melt and bond two layers of fabric with the heat of an iron.

Grainline: Indicated on a pattern by an arrow that aligns with the lengthwise or crosswise grain of the fabric.

High-loft fleece: Nonraveling fleece, usually made of polyester or polyester/Lycra blends; has a crosswise stretch. Use lightweight fleece for sportswear, blankets and craft items.

Interlock knit: A 1×1 knit construction like double knit, but lighter in weight. Interlocks are a little heavier than single knits. Interlocks are usually 100% cotton or a polyester/cotton blend, and have a soft hand. They stretch on the crosswise grain, but have little or no stretch on the lengthwise grain.

Jersey knit/single knit: Lightweight knits suitable for T-shirts, dresses, pull-on pants, shorts and sleepwear. They have 25–50% stretch and drape well. Single knits have flat, vertical ribs on the right side, and the opposite side resembles interlocking loops. Single knits curl to the right side when pulled on the crosswise grain.

Knit fabric: Fabric created by interlocking loops of yarn—one loop of yarn pulled through another loop. Most knits stretch. Examples of knit fabrics include interlock, sweatshirt fleece, sweater knits and more.

Knitted elastic: A soft, comfortable elastic that is specially knit with polyester and rubber fibers for extra stretch. It is available in several different sizes for swimwear, necklines, waistbands and leg bands.

Lettuce edge: A curly edge on ribbing or other stretchy knits. Use a narrow satin stitch on a sewing machine or a narrow rolled edge on a serger, and stretch the fabric in front of and in back of the presser foot as you are stitching to accomplish lettuce edging.

Lingerie/picot edge elastic: A ⅜" or ½" (10mm or 13mm) wide picot edge elastic used on lingerie and necklines for a lacy-looking edge.

Micro-serrated shears: Tiny teethlike grippers on the lower blade of these shears hold slippery knit fabrics, and the slightly blunted points prevent snagging fabric.

Multi-sized patterns: Patterns with several different sizes in one pattern; for example, sizes ranging from 8–12. Each pattern piece has cutting lines for all the sizes included in the pattern.

Multi-zigzag stitch: Variation of a machine zigzag stitch formed by sewing three stitches in each direction. It is often used when a stretch stitch or understitching is recommended.

Napped fabric: A fabric that has a loft or one-way texture. All sections of a napped fabric must be positioned in the same direction on a project.

Needle size: The higher the number, the heavier the needle. For example, a size 90/14 needle is heavier than a size 60/8 needle.

Nip: A ¼" (6mm) clip cut into a seam allowance prior to sewing. A nip marks a notch, dart, tuck, foldline or other important point on the fabric. A pattern notcher works well for this.

Notch(es): Single-, double- or triple-diamond markings found on sewing patterns that are used to match garment pieces accurately.

Overcast guide foot: A presser foot that creates smooth edge stitching without puckering. The overcast guide foot works well on knit seams when you are using knit stitches that overcast the edges.

Overlock: The most common stitch produced on a serger in which one or two needle threads are combined with an upper and lower looper instead of a bobbin. The overlock stitch is used to stitch seams with a serger, or to finish seams stitched on a conventional sewing machine.

Pattern notcher: A notion that looks similar to a paper punch with a spring action handle. The notcher is used to cut ⅟₁₆" × ¼" (2mm × 6mm) slits in your pattern pieces where triangular notches are located. The notcher is especially helpful for knit patterns because the clips are never longer than ¼" (6mm), so you won't accidently cut past a ¼" (6mm) seam allowance.

Pattern weights: Weighted items used to hold patterns in place on fabric.

Pile: The soft projecting fibers or nap on fabric, consisting of many small cut threads.

Pointelle knit: A lightweight openwork knit with a lacy effect.

Polyester: A synthetic or man-made fiber that can take on various characteristics depending on how it is processed. It may also be blended with other fibers such as cotton to produce a fabric with blended properties.

Quartermarks: Points indicated with pins or a washable marker to divide fabric into four equal parts. Quartermarks are used to position and distribute fabric evenly when sewing ribbing or elastic, for example, to the waist, neckline or the sleeves of a garment.

Raschel knit: A warp knit produced on a multiple-needle knitting machine. Lacelike, open-construction knit that resembles hand-crocheted fabric, lace and netting.

Ribbing: Ribbed knit fabric used to finish the neckline, waist and wrists of clothing.

Rotary cutter: Special fabric cutting tool that looks and works like a pizza cutter. Used in combination with a special cutting mat and gridded ruler, it is used to cut one or more layers of fabric accurately.

Ruffles: Fabric strips that are gathered or pleated by hand or machine and attached to another piece of fabric for a decorative frill or attached to the center of two pieces of fabric for a puffed heirloom embellishment.

Scallop stitch: Blind hem stitch used on the edge of a lightweight knit to produce a small scalloped edge or scallop stitch. The zigzag stitch made after a series of straight stitches pulls the knit fabric toward the straight stitches, forming the scallops.

Seam allowance: The distance from the stitching line to the cut edge of seamed fabrics. The most common seam allowance for knits is ¼" (6mm).

Seam sealant: Product used to seal the ends of fabric or thread to prevent raveling.

Serger: A special sewing machine that uses three, four or more threads instead of the two threads used on a conventional sewing machine. It features loopers to interlock the threads instead of a bobbin/bobbin case. It stitches a seam, finishes the raw edges, and trims the excess fabric all at the same time.

Slinky knit: Usually a blend of 90% acetate and 10% spandex. Spandex is added to slinky knits to keep them from bagging. Slinky knit is a very stretchy lightweight knit, with 100% stretch in the width and 50% in the length. It is comfortable to wear, drapes well and doesn't wrinkle—the ideal fabric for traveling.

Spandex: A synthetic fiber known for its exceptional stretch quality. A small percentage of these fibers are usually mixed with polyester or cotton when making knits for activewear.

Stabilizer: A material used to support the fabric and improve stitch quality during machine embroidery, appliqué and other embellishment on knits and wovens. Stabilizers are available in a variety of weights in cut-away, wash-away, heat-away and tear-away, as well as in liquid form.

Stitch in the ditch: Stitching on the front of a project in the well created by the seam to hold layers together. The stitching is virtually invisible.

Stretch needle: Needle designed with a medium ballpoint tip to prevent snags on knit fabric. Stretch needles come in various sizes to relate to the different weights of knit fabrics.

Stretch velour: A fabric made of knitted cotton or synthetic fibers; has a closely cropped pile on the right side. Stretch velour is fuzzy and warm, and may contain some spandex for a stretchy, comfortable fit.

Stretch velvet: A luxurious-looking fabric usually made of rayon or a rayon/silk blend with spandex for extra comfort and fit.

Sweatshirt fleece: A warm lightweight knit with very little stretch in either length or width. Fleece is usually a polyester/cotton blend, or 100% cotton. One side is brushed, and the other side has small, flat vertical ribs.

Swimwear: A two-way stretch knit, which stretches in both lengthwise and crosswise directions and has great stretch recovery. Usually made from a polyester/spandex blend.

Tear-away stabilizer: A stabilizer that can be removed from fabric by carefully tearing the stabilizer from around the design after embroidery is completed. Appropriate for dense stitching where tearing won't distort stitches or the fabric. May also be used as a "float" under the embroidery hoop for an additional layer of stabilizer when embroidering knits or wovens. Tear-away stabilizer may also be used for appliqué designs.

Textured nylon thread: Woolly-like thread used mainly in the loopers of a serger to give a soft, stretchy, ravel-free edgestitch, and for stitching fine very stretchy knits such as swimwear, lingerie, baby wear and activewear.

Thermal or waffle weave: 100% cotton square textured knit design retains heat. Used mostly for outerwear and underwear.

Topping: A stabilizer placed on the top of a fabric during machine embroidery, generally to prevent stitches from sinking into a napped base fabric, such as fleece.

Tricot knit: A lightweight warp knit, resistant to runs. This soft fine knit is used for lingerie and sportswear.

Two-way stretch knit: Any knit that has more than 25% stretch in both the crosswise and lengthwise directions. Knits will generally stretch more in the crosswise direction. Spandex and Lycra will often be part of the fiber content.

Understitch: Pressing seam allowances toward a facing or under collar, then stitching close to the seam on the facing to prevent the facing from rolling to the right side.

Warp knits: Fabric made with several yarns that are looped vertically at the same time. Many warp knits are produced on multiple needle knitting machines. Tricot and raschel knits are good examples of warp knits.

Wash-away double-sided tape: A basting tape for hard-to-pin fabrics. This ¼" (6mm) wide double-sided tape has a temporary adhesive to position zippers, pockets, trim and more. After stitching, wash out with water.

Wash-away stabilizer: A stabilizer designed for washable fabrics, or as a topping on knit fabrics with loft to prevent stitches from becoming embedded in the nap. Can be easily removed by spraying or immersing in water, leaving no visible residue.

Weft knits: Fabric made with a single yarn looped horizontally to form a row. Each row of a weft knit builds on the previous row, and may run when cut. Some examples of weft knits are single knits, double knits, ribbing and jersey.

Whipstitch: A hand stitch using heavy thread or yarn to overcast the edge of blankets and clothing, especially preferred for lightweight fleece.

Wobble stitch: A slight zigzag stitch for quilting. This stitch is also used for sewing knits because it allows the seams to stretch.

Zigzag stitch: A stitch that swings back and forth in a zigzag pattern to allow stitching to stretch with the fabric. A zigzag stitch may also be used for decorative stitching or appliqué.

Metric Conversion Chart

TO CONVERT	TO	MULTIPLY BY
Inches	Centimeters	2.54
Centimeters	Inches	0.4
Feet	Centimeters	30.5
Centimeters	Feet	0.03
Yards	Meters	0.9
Meters	Yards	1.1

Measurements have been given in imperial inches with metric conversions in parentheses. Use one or the other as they are not interchangeable. The most accurate results will be obtained using inches.

Index

fw media www.fwmedia.com

17 16 15 14 13   5 4 3 2 1

DISTRIBUTED IN CANADA BY FRASER DIRECT
100 Armstrong Avenue
Georgetown, ON, Canada L7G 5S4
Tel: (905) 877-4411

DISTRIBUTED IN THE U.K. AND EUROPE BY F&W MEDIA INTERNATIONAL
Brunel House, Newton Abbot, Devon, TQ12 4PU, England
Tel: (+44) 1626 323200, Fax: (+44) 1626 323319
Email: enquiries@fwmedia.com

DISTRIBUTED IN AUSTRALIA BY CAPRICORN LINK
P.O. Box 704, S. Windsor NSW, 2756 Australia
Tel: (02) 4577-3555

ISBN-13: 978-1-4402-3033-2
SRN: W8767

Edited by Stefanie Laufersweiler
Designed by Anna Fazakerley
Production coordinated by Greg Nock
Photographed by Jack Kirby and Jack Gorman
Illustrations by Laure Noe
Nancy's Notions editorial staff: Diane Dhein and Pat Hahn

About the Author

Nancy Zieman is executive producer and host of Public TV's long-running *Sewing With Nancy,* where she has been teaching viewers the art of sewing, quilting and embroidering since 1982. She also founded Nancy's Notions, a mail-order and online source for sewing and quilting products. As one of the sewing industry's most trusted voices, she has been honored and celebrated by organizations from 4-H to the American Sewing Guild. So, wherever you see a *Note from Nancy,* you'll know you're getting expert advice!

Acknowledgments

As the figurehead of a TV show and direct mail company, I tend to receive undeserved accolades for the successes of both entities. The proverb that includes the words "it takes a village" applies to life in general. My village is a tight-knit group of people who have worked with me over many decades. My TV program should really be called *Sewing With Nancy, Donna, Pat, Laure, Kate, Diane D., Diane S., Deanna, Lois, Denise and Erica.* They comprise the dedicated village that shares a love of sewing and quilting. To them I extend my appreciation and give a heartfelt thank you for being loyal members of my team and great friends.

Fabric you love, supplies you need, books that inspire…

Visit **store.MarthaPullen.com**

You'll find everything you need to start and complete a successful sewing project—and you don't even have to leave the house! Visit store.MarthaPullen.com for all the fabrics, threads, tools and notions you need, and check out these additional titles from Nancy Zieman for valuable instruction and endless inspiration.

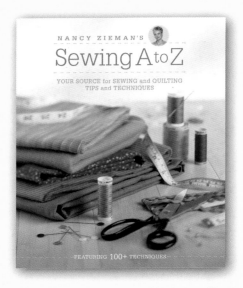

Nancy Zieman's Sewing A to Z
Your Source for Sewing and Quilting Tips and Techniques

Whether you're a novice sewer or a skilled seamstress, who better to go to for sewing answers and advice than expert Nancy Zieman? Set aside your sewing fears and let Nancy guide you step-by-step through 100+ basic to advanced sewing methods and techniques. Covering alphabetized topics ranging from Appliqué to Zippers, Nancy will help you achieve beautiful results with every project.

Nancy's Favorite 101 Notions
Sew, Quilt and Embroider with Ease

For the past 25 years, Nancy Zieman has offered innovative ideas, inspiration and information designed to make sewing, serging, quilting and embroidering more efficient—and more enjoyable. Now she offers a guidebook to every tool you'll ever need! In it, Nancy describes the features of each tool—from standards to one-task wonders—and details its various uses. Find the tools that will make sewing easier, faster, more creative and more fun!